MEDITATIONS ON SAINT LUKE

ORBIS BOOKS
Maryknoll, New York 10545

MEDITATIONS ON SAINT LUKE

ARTURO PAOLI

TRANSLATED BY
BERNARD F. McWILLIAMS, C.SS.R.

Originally published in 1972 as *La radice dell'uomo. Meditazioni sul vangelo di Luca.* © 1972 by Ed. Morcelliana, Brescia, Italy

The English translation is based on the revised Spanish edition: *La perspectiva política de san Lucas.* © 1974 by Siglo XXI de España Editores, S.A., Madrid, and Siglo XXI Argentina Editores, S.A., Buenos Aires

English translation © 1977 by Orbis Books, Maryknoll, New York 10545

Printed in the United States of America

Library of Congress Cataloging in Publication Data

Paoli, Arturo.
    Meditations on Saint Luke.

    Rev. translation of La radice dell'uomo, originally published in 1972.
    1. Bible. N.T. Luke—Meditations. I. Title.
BS2595.4.P3313   1977   225'.4'06   76-58539
ISBN 0-88344-314-7
ISBN 0-88344-315-5 pbk.

CONTENTS

1

Where the Road Ends

They were childless, for Elizabeth was sterile; moreover, both were advanced in years (Lk 1,7).

Human salvation occurs in an encounter: God and the desert; fullness and sterility. The barren land resounds with the voice of a woman. Sarah laughs inside the tent at the thought of her aged Abraham engendering a child (Gn 18, 9–19). Zechariah doubts the word of promise, and so becomes mute during the long months of waiting for John. The river of life, capable of irrigating the land, fertilizes the womb of a woman.

I am reading Luke's pages in a desert, a rock-strewn desert bounded to the south by mountains whose seductive colors change with the changing light of the day. But it is impossible to yield to the temptation to explore, for we are separated from the mountains by a wild area of wadis and gulches apparently carved by waters long since swallowed up by the earth. To the north there is a small strip of vegetation, dying of thirst. A murmuring stream—the only sound in the total silence—flows uselessly through devastated vineyards and ruined orchards, eating away at the foundations of abandoned houses. Farther on, there is the stony bed of a river, but without any water. On the other bank the scorched earth begins. The few people who survive here must cross the sandy terrain and go upriver daily in search of water for themselves and their animals—water to drink, to wash in, and to break open the dark skin of the land.

Dazzled by the brightness, one's eyes see what is at once an Eden and a desert. And they see people who live suspended between the promises of life and the active presence of death. To the west the road vanishes among the rocks, pointing to the only possibility of escape to the distant city before the remaining walls crumble and the doors, made by hands that knew of beauty, fall into the rubble. This is Suriyaco, my desert.

Here, in this setting, I think about my times, my culture, my struggling generation. I reflect upon our age—productive and yet sterile, esthetic yet incapable of contemplating beauty, violently bent on revolution and yet incapable of salvation, straining toward the future but threatened by the present. It is an age that seems without hope because it lacks *grace*. It is the epilogue of the "patriarchal" era, where "life" means reproduction and the ideal is to sow a seed in the womb of a woman, or in the womb of the earth, or in the womb of a bank, so that it will multiply. Life, growth, is a question of numbers, of quantitative multiplication.

The history of nature involves the history of the person, which is constituted by design for the future, choice, new creation. In the heart of the technological economy sterility appears. The contemplation of beauty that leads to adoration, the search for self-identity, communication that should issue in communion—it all ends in a desert of stone. Some of our young people find themselves in this hopeless desert and try to alert the rest. Insofar as we discover our meaning in the world, our being as part of things, our world begins to become strange and hostile for us. Every day we become increasingly aware that it is in a state of alienation. "Yes, we know that all creation groans and is in agony even until now" (Rom 8,22). This quotation from Romans is from a context where Paul is speaking of liberation from fear and the security of persons who feel they are on the right road. . . . "You did not receive a spirit of slavery leading you back into fear, but a spirit of adoption through which we cry out, 'Abba!' (that is, 'Father')" (Rom 8,15). The fundamental projection of the person into the future coincides with a liberation from fear, and consequently from aggressiveness toward nature. The "economic" attitude is clearly the most violent; it is the immediate cause of violence among people and the sterility of nature.

Here in this valley there has been no war as such, there was no barbarian invasion; but the "capitalists" marched through. The beauty here has been destroyed by economic violence. The ravaged earth, instead of protecting the person, can only inspire fear.

Before we can talk about peace among nations and people, it is necessary to talk about peace between people and things. Human violence against nature is "economic" violence, and today it is called capitalism, a term that means a freezing of our wealth so that it can be transformed from "beauty" and "communion" into "security" and "separation." This aggressive violence generates, like offspring, fear and sterile and impotent estheticism that is a parody of contemplation. It is the one sign of a capacity for wonder that the culture of technology is able to produce, and it masks a fundamental inability really to enjoy beauty. It is in a void, without roots in the earth, quantitative, not qualitative, because the capitalist culture does not restore things. It restores only their form, the empty image, not the reality. Thus jet planes take people, in need of beauty to survive, from the Pyramids to the city of the Incas, from Chartres to Niagara Falls; but all these images flow past dazed eyes without these people getting to the heart of things. Things remain without heart for them—without essence, without life, alienated. For this reason people go from the Prado to the volcanoes of Japan and to the Neapolitan coast without experiencing the interior change connoting "love," "project," "communion." Things become their enemies.

In *Zabriskie Point*, a film by Antonioni, nature is sought in the flight from the big capitalist metropolis; beautiful at first sight, it is changed into a dark valley where earthen creatures are coupling. All these worm-people are equal; they seem to reproduce themselves in a frightening and vertiginous way. The joy of birth, of life, is swallowed up by this awesome multiplication; each pair shows signs of lacking a design for communion and, as a result, the joy of existing. Before this creature who emerges from the desert, buildings become cardboard scenery, theatrical facades which, when an explosion takes place, sail through the air, multiplying themselves like the creatures on the valley floor. People and pieces of wood and cardboard are blown to bits, like the grand finale of a fireworks display. Prior to this spectacular finale—more a theater of puppets than a human habitat—the cameras make a slow pass over the perfection of detail of a health spa built on a rock where they have reproduced artificially the most exquisite examples of feminine beauty.

The contemplative attitude is completely distinct from estheticism, bastard child of capitalism. Contemplation matures in communion with Brother Fire, with Sister Water, with Brother Wolf and discovers a loving and joyful brotherhood, whereas estheticism ends up in visual pleasure and estrangement, without getting us out of our loneliness. Contemplation provokes a reaction of "how good it is to be here. Let us erect three booths. . . . " Estheticism demands succession, change. The contemplative design for the future is qualitative change, reconciliation with things. The universe is discovered to be liberated from slavery and weakness in order to take part in the "glorious freedom of the children of God" (Rom 8,21).

Things welcome contemplatives as if they were coming home, reconciled. Esthetes do not ask to be accepted by things, they are not one with them, they dominate things violently from the outside; instead of brothers and sisters they are conquerors. Esthetes think they see beauty, but they fail to because they do not possess it, do not enter into it. They see it only with their eyes and not with their whole being. In order to enter into beauty, possess it, we must come unarmed; we must be peacemakers. We must stand before creation to be received by it; otherwise we will be shut off. And to be received, we must begin by acknowledging that we have lost the right to be in the Father's house and to enjoy his things. . . . Our generation has taken a forward step, with respect to the generation of estheticism. The form has been swallowed by the movement. We are in the Exodus; and when we remain still we find that we are in the desert. Youth searches for beauty but rejects the "beauty produced by the system." In its anxious quest of beauty it rejects estheticism. Young people know intuitively that technology cannot lead us to the contemplation of beauty; it is an anticontemplative culture, and for this reason destructive of the beautiful. Loneliness has its roots here: We are loners, swimming in existence like fish, aware of being in the sea but not penetrated by the water. We are alone in the great sea of being because being does not touch us and we do not know how to relate to each other. We do not feel ourselves to be "with" others, but "above" and "against" them, and with a utilitarian finality.

Contemplatives find themselves contemplated, identified, with a look that explains their unique and unrepeatable existence; and at the same time they are among and with other beings. It is a look that liberates them from a careless and superficial curiosity and enables them to penetrate to the very roots of existence: "Hear me, O coastlands, listen, O distant peoples. The Lord called me from birth, from my mother's womb he gave me my name" (Is 49,1). "Before I formed you in the womb, I knew you, before you were born I dedicated you, a prophet to the nations I appointed you" (Jer 1,5).

I know intuitively that nobody possesses more of beauty, nobody goes deeper into the meaning of creation, than those who discover that their personal life is painfully charged with meaning—meaning that has its roots in their personhood and at the same time outside it; in their era, yet outside their history and above it.

Those who discover their meaning—a meaning in themselves, in their own existence—do not ask it of things, either by violence or by stirring up piety. They are with things that have meaning before them and after them, a meaning that has the same origin and the same cause as they do. We should rediscover a meaning that is *in* us, whereas our culture has accustomed us to look for it *outside* us, in the esthetic and the economic. In a succession of havings and seeings, our motion is not in obedience to the meaning that is within us; it is not the historicization of a calling, but a displacing of ourselves to change the view, so that others can give us the feeling of existing.

Into this very same destiny enter the two dialogues essential to us: dialogue with God and dialogue with the person. Is dialogue with God possible without poverty? God is not "economic," God is gratuitous. When our prayer became "economic," "capitalist," pageantry and estheticism became a part of our prayer. Prayer, before it is put into words, is a state of being. Being religious is not the performance of acts or the return of things loaned to us by God; it is obedience to a historic destiny that is personal and, at the same time, communal. Beauty is the purpose of history; peace, harmony, unity, music are different words that express the same reality. To be religious is to give your life so that the world may be more beautiful, more just, more at peace; it is to prevent egotistical and self-serving ends from disrupting this harmony of the whole. Contemplatives are religious. Drawn toward the roots of being, they rediscover the meaning of things; and in the meaning of their names and of their existence among others in time, they discover the true meaning of history . . . "From my mother's womb he gave me my name." And revolutionaries are religious; they do not accept the existing order, they refuse to live a life without meaning, and they struggle to re-create a social reality whose thrust shall be toward living together in love and in the constant search for dignity in the other.

Apart from these limits, religion is an expression of fear, a mask of self-interest, idolatry. Religion does not take us out of the desert; it seals us off in crystallized historical forms and prevents us from hearing the original and personal call of God. Religion has only one dimension: the encounter with God in the nakedness of being, at the root of existence. In that dimension I discover my own identity as well as those beings with whom I share creaturehood, producing in this way a loving, happy, wholesome encounter. And sinking roots into this wholesomeness demands the courage to accept the world as being in a process of constant creation in which things go on being liberated from human aggressiveness.

Religion cannot be reduced to models or schemata. When it is said: "The family is no longer . . . ," "Youth is no longer . . . ," "Nations are no longer . . . ," what is implied is "as before," as in an ideal but nonexistent time. A model is chosen, the liberating power of God is crystallized in an imaginary stage, in a mold I have fabricated for myself. Faith and hope can only be transmitted when they truly animate my own life. We can teach prayer only when it is a part of our life, and then only in a dialogue of real and deep friendship. "Few things that I have been ordered to do under obedience have given me more difficulty than to speak now about prayer," wrote Saint Teresa. Prayer as we find it today does not draw us out of the desert of our sterility, since it is the expression of people hardened in their economic and esthetic options—that is to say, aggressive.

Nothing, or almost nothing, can be said about prayer because prayer, in itself, does not exist. Jesus, in the Gospel, speaks about a man of prayer who shut himself up in his room in order "to be seen" only by the Father. He does not say many words, because the Father is aware of his situation. He remains in an attitude of silence because he should not explain the meaning of events to someone who already knows their meaning; rather he himself should understand this meaning in its full depth. When the disciples insist that Jesus teach them to pray, he gives them three basic concepts to follow: *the will of the Father*, that is, to rediscover the meaning of life in its origin, in the root of their existence, as the reason for their being. They are not to expect this from outside themselves in the unfolding of events. *To struggle so that the kingdom of God will come*, so that beauty shall be discovered, so that harmony shall become greater harmony, peace greater peace, until the encounter with the One. *Communion among people*, to forgive those who hurt us, to accept the human condition in all its consequences.

The hippies search for contemplation apart from the surrounding culture, as an activity that is born and consummated within people themselves. Although this can be an escape, a denial of the revolutionary struggle to free the world—and it is difficult to dismiss this charge—in their approach is to be found the freshness of an original and authentic meaning of prayer.

Persons have meaning in themselves; events that happen, living among other people—these help us to decipher the meaning. This meaning is not outside of history but very much within it. Jeremiah discovers that he is a sign of contradiction in the history of his people and involved in a terrible conflict: "Remember me, Lord, visit me, and avenge me on my persecutors; . . . know that for you I have borne insult." And in his profound depression he discovered the principle, the root, of his existence: "When I found your words, I devoured them; they became my joy and the happiness of my heart" (Jer 15,15–16). Our generation is incapable of being religious because it is incapable of this kind of wonder, incapable of experiencing the joy of just being; and for this reason our joys do not run deep and do not touch the heart of the person. It is naive to blame everything on distractions; these are nothing more than a projection of the one and only distraction. Nothing is more irreligious than to give to distracted people religious forms and expressions that are only an echo of their distraction; to treat them as children to whom you have to talk of "other things" while trying to get them to take their medicine. The most alienating kind of religion is that which permits people to fulfill their "religious duties" without abandoning their distractions. The religious act, in effect, becomes one more in a series of distractions. The very ones who arrange to give distracted people a religion energetically reject many projects that could liberate them and separate them from their great distraction. Underneath these efforts to make the fulfillment of religious duties easier for distracted people is the concept of an Egyptian god, installed on his throne and awaiting our worship.

The only sign of being "touched by God" is to be able to see yourself as "universal brother"—to use a favorite phrase of Father De Foucauld's. And this means to be in communion with people and with all beings. Where this communion is not present, the mark of the Christian is to take on the fight and face death so that this communion will come about. The New Testament speaks of prayer as thanksgiving. The Christian liturgy is called the Eucharist, that is, gratitude, the pleasure of "being well." In terms of the concept of the Egyptian god, the expression "thanks be to God" seems degrading to God and to ourselves. Our "God willing" is an expression of self-interest and fear more than of contemplation. But Eucharist is the very existential condition of those who know they are accepted by others and share in their destiny. "And now, brothers, I beg you through the mercy of God to offer your bodies as a living sacrifice holy and acceptable to God, your spiritual worship" (Rom 12,1).

Prayer is entreaty because it expresses our anguish, our dualism, our difficulty with relating to being, and therefore the temptation to get out from under our difficult position; but prayer tends to become gratitude. The economic, as a category apart, separate from the human, depersonalized, is the opposite of thanksgiving; it is anti-eucharistic. Whereas the Eucharist is the sign of integration among humans, of acceptance among the others, the economic is a sign of separateness, of the draining off, by an economic group, of the blood that circulates through the body of humanity in order to give it unity. Are we really "economic" beings, or should we act economically? To become enmeshed in the accumulation-distribution-consumption economy—is this a phase of our identity, or is it a result of our being-with-others, an authentic sign of our identity? Here, I think, is the root of the problem posed by our culture: in other words, can a Christian be "economic" in the sense that our culture gives to the word? We should consider, from this very deep level, the incompatibility proclaimed in Matthew's sixth chapter: "You cannot give yourself to God and money." The meaning of persons does not come from their economic function but from their being with others, in a state of creative tension, with the end of bringing about a progressive perfectioning of this being-together, a fullness of communion. For this reason the Christian rite is called "Eucharist" and "Communion." They are two moments of prayer, and at the same time, two moments of the rhythm of life in the person. "Sharing among humans," writes Paul Ricoeur, "is not possible without an awareness of *taking part in a creative theme* that sets the tone and gives meaning to the community, conferring upon it a bond and an end; it is always an Idea that gives meaning to the growth of a 'we' and of 'friendship' " (*Finitude et culpabilité*, p. 120). If accumulation, distribution, and consumption have as an end this growth and this friendship, then although I may be governed by economic laws and make use of technical know-how, I am not for this reason transformed into a *homo oeconomicus*. Moreover when consumption—which is our most violent act—is not destructive and violent, but rather a respectful communion with things, it is transformed into a eucharistic act, that is, thanksgiving. Grace before and after meals is a mockery if it does not express this profound communion.

Anti-eucharistic society posts sickening menus, as for the rich and rare dishes served overindulged jet travellers or the patrons of fashionable restaurants. These delicacies are the droppings of birds of prey. Eating such meals represents not an affectionate communion of people with things, a reciprocal acceptance; rather it means a violent incursion upon things that are good and beautiful. I was thinking about this while putting some notes in order after having dined with a tribe of Makiritar Indians in their community house. One of them gave me a piece of meat he had begun to chew on and a slice of cassava dipped in a sauce. This frugal meal of the poor, where communion, being together, far exceeded the menu in abundance, is projected in my mind against a background of other boring meals where the refined manners, the conventional behavior, attempted in vain to hide a total lack of human warmth.

We must rethink prayer in this richness of motive; there is nothing new about stating that we are as we pray and we pray as we are. The aggressiveness of people against people, the problem of war—these are not to be resolved with a psychological gesture, with a sentimental formalism adopted in the moment of prayer. We must consider with greater seriousness and at greater depth the phrase of the gospel: "If you bring your gift to the altar and there recall that your brother has anything against you, leave your gift at the altar, go first to be reconciled with your brother, and then come and offer your gift" (Mt 5,23–24). It does not say, "If you have anything against your brother," but "If your brother has anything against you." And we should understand by this not only a grudge, a feeling of hatred, but also a situation of violence that makes another suffer and for which I am responsible, a situation of oppression and injustice for which I am at least partially to blame. Prayer that does not embrace things is not Christian. Christian prayer is "in things." "Praised be my Lord for my Sister Water, for my Brother Wind, for my Brother Fire." Not only praised *because* God has given us water, fire, and wind but praised by means of water, in water, in fire, in wind. We cannot pray unless we are reconciled with all our brothers and sisters, and among them it is necessary to include all creatures: wind, fire, wheat, bread, copper, gold, oil.

Declarations in favor of peace sound hollow even when they are made with the best of intention. They refer to peace as though it were a psychological decision, a choice carried out by human beings behind the back of things and structures. Peace is the search for justice, and the primary form of justice is the recognition that we are creatures among creatures with a responsibility for creation. To many—especially to young people—religion has come to be regarded as an easy way to avoid the painful search for identity and the advent of a method of communicating that will not come about by itself but must be worked at. People today do not pray, because they feel that prayer without reconciliation among people is spurious. A relationship with God can be authentic only if a person is either a contemplative or a revolutionary. There is no incompatibility between these two forms of expression: The contemplative should be a revolutionary and the revolutionary should be a contemplative. Religious people cannot be led to contemplation unless they energetically reject our economic society. If they allow themselves to become entangled in its very subtle mesh, they are guilty of violence against things, they are not reconciled, they are not creatures among creatures; they are objects of consumption and not subjects of creation according to the plan of God. Revolutionaries are those who do not accept the structure, who try to shatter a false image of the person, formed in an unjust society. They too, like the contemplatives, search along another way for an existentially ontological truth. They look for the *real* person—that is, freed from alienations. Revolutionaries will become fatally stranded in the desert of sterility if, in destroying structures, they do not see the "new person," if they do not look for the liberated person, that is, the real person. Religion will become stranded in the desert of sterility if it offers "economic" people *things*, abetting their need for excitement, novelty, estheticism; if it leads them on to an extending of themselves rather than to a deepening.

There is a certain pseudo-progressive pastoral approach designed to provide workers travelling to their jobs with well-packaged food to save them the trouble of stopping for lunch; and, yes, the approach is ridiculed as cheap publicity in spite of the fact that it seems to fill the need of some groups who welcome the food. An unforeseen result is that religious people have felt themselves reduced to the status of travelling salesmen, displayers of industrial products. This crisis would not have happened without the advent of a search for religious authenticity that challenges an easy and comfortable religion not committed to people in history. Contemplatives have nothing to distribute, but they rediscover the meaning of the person in an intense destiny of love and risk, whose ultimate demand is to lay down your life for your friends. And this destiny is not tragic, because at the moment when we see ourselves as a project of love with others and for others, the existence of love is revealed to us.

The liberation of history from the structures that reduce the person to *homo oeconomicus* has to be sustained by the certain hope that once the shell of technological civilization is cracked, we will come alive and exist as beings capable of love, since we are loved; that things, freed of the winding-sheet of technology, will exist as "created"—that is to say, "loved"—and capable, therefore, of receiving persons into their midst and giving them joy. This is essential joy that gives substance and tone to all the other joys we experience: the joy of existing and not being alone; of being "with," of being "among," and of being "for." Contemplatives do not give formulas; they do not give things. They radiate a joy that needs no support from without; that is not conditioned by events to come, but rises from within like a fountain of living water: This is their marvelling at existence. Happiness is to feel loved; there is an indestructible link between "being" and "being loved."

We have ended up in the desert: the desert of noncommunication with things, with God, and with the other. Economic culture could not have had any other epilogue than making a thing out of a person. The rhythm of the economic person is accumulation-distribution-consumption, whereas the rhythm of love is to give of oneself, to lose the self in order to grow and to rediscover the self. But the absence of love in economic persons fills them with such gnawing anxiety that they are pushed into making desperate decisions that can have the appearance of acts of love. Saint Paul unmasks this subterfuge of egoism and fear and sets if forth in a famous text: "If I give everything I have to feed the poor and hand over my body to be burned, but have not love, I gain nothing" (1 Cor 13,3). Our economic culture has made us incapable of thinking beyond economic categories; everything is regarded as negotiable property, whereas love is outside these economic categories. The body is bought and sold, but not love. The lack of love reduces economic persons to desperation, but it doesn't make them humble. Desperation because they lack the one essential good, the only one that gives substance and savor to all the other goods. They feel more miserable than the poor, the oppressed, who lack "worldly goods" but who more often than not have the "good." "If I have not love, I am nothing."

There is no remedy for their pain because they never manage to free themselves from the category of the economic. They see love as a right, on a par with their automobile, their house, and the services their employees render them. I have frequently heard the disillusioned rich cry out that they have been cheated—the kind of insolence you would never hear from the poor person. The rich people have paid for the full-course dinner, dessert and cover charge included—why are they not served love? Accustomed to the mathematical efficiency of money and its exactness, to the instant response they get when they order people about, they do not even suspect that they can be rejected or that all their offers of "love" can be spurned, leaving them all alone. The true aristocracy of the poor, their truly mighty power—greater than economic or military power—is the power to *reject*, to "close the doors." "What I say to you is this," we read in Luke's gospel: "Make friends for yourselves through your use of this world's goods, so that when they fail you, a lasting reception will be yours" (Lk 16,9). I don't know of a counsel in all the gospel more risky and complicated than this one, although it seems so simple. Its riskiness is rooted in the fact that it is a saying that has the structure, simple in the extreme, of the economic mechanism of the offer to pay and the demand to receive: I pay and I demand; that which I pay for should be delivered to me without fail. We cannot isolate the problem of love and communication between two people from the larger problem of communion with people and things. We would not know where to begin; the new person must be born of the destruction of the economic person. We must be re-created through friendship and the love that it is not found within the framework of the economic person because it is incompatible with it. The first act of humility of the economic person, the sign of conversion, would be to admit this incompatibility.

It is true that love between two people, the love of friendship, is difficult on all social levels; the lack of love and the failure to love exist equally in the world of the rich and in the world of the poor. It is clear that the difficulty in loving is not a special sickness of the rich. The wealthy woman is just as boxed-in as the lower-class woman, in a different way but with the same results. This observation can bring us to the conclusion that it is useless to change structures, stamp out capitalist culture from the world, because the deeper evil resides in the person, in sin. Therefore the most urgent reform, and perhaps the only one really needed, would be the reform of the person, interior conversion, which in the end is the only reform about which the gospel speaks clearly. But can we be reformed if we continue to project our monstrous egoism in a social and political structure? And would not the sign of our conversion be a political and social creation inspired by communion instead of isolation? We are unable to think of persons divorced from the structures we project, our political and social profile. For this reason it seems to me idle to speak of priority or of antithesis: First let us change persons, and their social projections will come as a consequence. Nevertheless for many centuries "converted" persons have been appearing on the scene, persons supposedly in a state of grace, who have been responsible for ugly political and economic structures of oppression and lack of love. Paul Ricoeur asks himself this question:

Should we say that innocence in possessing is unthinkable, that to possess was wrong from the beginning and that *human communion* is possible only at the price of renouncing totally the right to possess? Certain historical forms of appropriation are undoubtedly incompatible with total reconciliation; the Socialist critique of the nineteenth century has great meaning in this respect (*Finitude et culpabilité*, p. 131).

Because of my faith in the gospel I feel that the solution is contained, like a mineral in rock, in the phrase: "Make friends for yourselves so that a lasting reception will be yours." If interpreted in the economic sense, this injunction can give rise to horrendous misapprehensions: little orphans attending Mass for the repose of the soul of the capitalist benefactor; solemn funerals that come at a high price; opulent foundations funded by money robbed from the poor—all this seems to be authorized by a phrase that has the sound of a banking transaction. Nevertheless it is enough to ponder the entire meaning of the phrase to see that it is as explosive as the Copernican revolution. It is the poor who are to accept you as friends and to open their doors to you. It is not said that they would do this for you because you offered them something that you believe to be a sign of friendship. To you, the rich, it seems obvious. That the president of the United States or the winner of the Nobel prize for chemistry would become my friend is not very probable. But a poor person, a beggar, a farmhand who cleans out the stables? That would be all I need. . . . Nevertheless that's what happens. You have managed to become friends of the U.S. president because you have invited him to tea on your yacht. But you have not been able to become a friend to that woman over there who is looking at you, half surprised and half terrified. It is the poor and the marginally poor who have power over that part of me where love resides, and therefore over my essential happiness that I cannot renounce without renouncing life itself. The gospel goes very deep, indicating, probably, the revolutionary attitude: *Give the decision-making power to the poor, to the oppressed.* They are the ones who should decide, who should give acceptance.

Economic persons have projected into the spiritual realm their very elemental plan, simple as a law of mathematics, in which things work out in heaven in the same way they do on earth; heaven is bought as if it were the earth. On earth government officials, municipal administrators, labor leaders are bought. In heaven the poor are bought. And also the orphans, the prisoners, the refugees enter into my history as the faceless consumers of oil, cotton, copper, allowing me to journey as a tourist to as many islands as there are in the Pacific.

The realignment of values that the gospel makes is truly revolutionary, and there is much irony in it. It strips from those who hold power unlawfully the most important decision, that which concerns the very center of one's being. Faced with the power of the capitalist structure of a rich nation, we ask ourself how we are to escape from the net: the economy, public relations, politics—everything is rigidly controlled and ably directed. Nevertheless these executive directors are not able to produce the only values that are truly human, those of communication and of love. The "lasting reception" spoken of in the gospel is not a reward given to the worker on retiring, or a trip to the theater for the student who has gotten good grades; it is the discovery that we have hit upon what is real and permanent and essential and no one can take it away from us. The arrival point will be the clear revelation that we have been on the right road: "Now we see indistinctly as in a mirror; then we shall see face to face. My knowledge is imperfect now; then I shall know even as I am known" (1 Cor 13,12).

The decision is in the hands of the poor, and it is a decision that is active, conscious, human: "Make friends for yourselves so that a lasting reception will be yours." In this sphere the poor do not serve as an economic datum to be kept in mind when projecting the gross product and its reception by consumers: How many are there? Where are they? What kind of marketing psychology can we reach them with? No, anyone who does not love and is not loved in return is not received.

From this point of view the human condition seems even more complicated and dramatic, because the solution to the deepest problem facing us, that of communication, is not to be found in a kind of psychological determination, in a "movement of the soul," in a decision made between God and myself; I must settle accounts with whoever has me at their disposal. The great power of wealth, which has at its disposal the world and all its activity and trafficking, finds itself paralyzed before this obstacle which it had not even considered. I can dispose of my goods and of my very self, but I cannot decide whether I will be a person or not, a person or a non-person. This decision is in the hands of the voiceless ones: They will decide whether to accept me as a friend or to reject me.

The words of the First Epistle to the Corinthians are seen in a new light: "If I speak with human tongues and angelic as well, but do not have love, I am a noisy gong, a clanging cymbal. If I have the gift of prophecy and, with full knowledge, comprehend all mysteries, if I have faith great enough to move mountains, but have not love, I am nothing. If I give everything I have to feed the poor and hand over my body to be burned, but have not love, I gain nothing" (1 Cor 13,1–3). The decision to love must be made by the others—the poor, those I have offended, those I have treated unjustly. Thus a sense of limitation, which industrial society lacks, is introduced through this door in its structure. Spatial and temporal limitations are interiorized, made more human. I don't know how we can resolve this problem, which is the historic theme of our generation; but not knowing how to solve it should not make us ignore it as if it were something that did not concern us.

The world in which we live seems like a scene from an Albee play. The couple who occupy a house in a rich neighborhood feel as if they have been suddenly thrown out. Who is the intruder who has entered their house and refuses to live with them? Nobody. They are both seized with a strange fear, bodiless and faceless. It is someone who is stronger than any homeowner, stronger than any conquering nation; it is someone who does not accept them who throws them out. It is the history of the world. We cannot help thinking of the gospel phrase "To his own he came, yet his own did not accept him" (Jn 1,11). They have not accepted the Friend because he is poor and trustworthy, and the economic persons are thrown out of their house by this strange and powerful master who is poor. Christ identified him when he said (Mt 25, 37): "I was hungry and you gave me to eat." . . . "When did we see you hungry?" Those who ask this question have certainly given alms, shared what they have; but they have not seen the *person.* *"When did we see you?"* It would seem as if proportionately with our economic growth and our conquest of the universe, our lack of communication and our isolation increase.

Seen from this perspective of the gospel, the world seems incurable because those in power are ready for anything, ready to strip themselves completely: The pain of loneliness is so unbearable that the cost of being set free from it never becomes high enough. They are prepared to do anything except to beg the poor to accept them or to let the poor make the decisions. Every cry for peace, for coexistence among people and nations, has a hollow sound because it appeals to the responsibility and good will of those in power. An effort is made to convince them, with threats or with flattery, that the problem of peace is a problem of good will. The powerful come out of conferences and summit meetings convinced that the ability to bring about peace in the world is in their hands. The United Nations, the churches, the law-makers have persuaded them that peaceful coexistence in the world depends on them and that it is up to them whether to be a good neighbor or not, whether to communicate or not with neighboring nations. Their situation worsens because they feel compelled to inflate their power and make it seem more astute, more circumspect, more technically efficient.

In every meeting of the bourgeoisie that I have ever attended, the deep thinkers, urged on by an analysis of a world without peace and without communication, have asked themselves the question "What to do?" Indeed, one group has actually named itself "What To Do?" Another: "And Now?" Bourgeois Christians expect me, as the speaker, to stir up within them the anguish of thinking that "we Christians are the reason the world is badly off." To be honest, I should really say to them: You can do nothing. This is not the place where decisions of peace and coexistence are made. This is not a deliberative organ. You lack power and authority. We have all made a big mistake. We thought that "historic groups"—that is, groups with a capacity to move, to transform the world, to go forward—were the same as power groups. The training given by religious people is responsible for this mistake, and now the consequences are taking their toll. The answers that come out of these meetings stutter, stumble, and slip in the night. The surer we seem to be of the answers, the more we sink into the swamp of loneliness and noncommunication. Open up a leprosarium in the Congo, a school in Matto Grosso. Send a plane loaded with chocolate to Biafra. . . .

It never occurs to anyone to bring together the *deliberative organ* that really has the power to make decisions. Certainly it is much easier to round up a group of "aware" people who are ready to help others. But these people have the power to "give," not to "receive," whereas the gospel speaks inexorably of receiving.

"Make friends so that they will receive you." It is fitting that those who are not welcome in the office of the first-rate dentist, or in the study of the distinguished lawyer, or in hospitals run by the Blue Nuns or the Grey Nuns, no longer wish to be welcomed. The condition of the world is incurable because we neither understand nor accept the import of this passage in the gospel. Artists like Pasolini try to make the theme contemporary, clothing it in violence and eroticism, but the economic generation sees nothing more in that than obscenity. Revolutionary groups try to turn the situation around, giving to the poor and the outcasts of the world not more of something but the power to decide; and then those who lament their loneliness and weep over the tragic destiny of humankind oppose the change with all their resources. They condemn as subversive any movement designed to turn things around.

But we must make up our minds; either we accept things as they are—stoically putting up with war, fear, noncommunication, rejection—and admit that history is a matter of power, a search for the balance of power among nations; or we refuse to accept the established order and struggle for power to be given to the poor. We are not talking about a mechanical upheaval, of an automatic changing of the guard, which would obviously leave things as bad as before, if not worse. We are talking about a cultural change, one in which wealth would no longer be a symbol of fear and of power, but a symbol of friendship.

The church proclaimed prophetically, in *Populorum Progressio,* the need to discover new techniques and to bring about a thorough renewal. The only hope for the world is to be sought in those who no longer expect solutions from those who consider themselves the protagonists in the human drama because they hold power in their hands. It is necessary to engage in this search with humility and courage. It is necessary to have the courage of one facing the uncharted, the unknown; and this courage will come to our generation partly because it believes that the risen Christ is mysteriously guiding our history and partly because the sicknesses—loneliness, noncommunication, rejection—which extend to all sectors have become unbearable.

The generations bearing blood and holiness, heroism and cowardice, faith and unfaithfulness, come to a term in the sterile womb of Elizabeth. The lineage that God had promised to multiply "like grains of sand and like the stars of heaven" is brought together in order to die in the womb of that old woman. The "chosen" people, responsible for preserving the thread of hope through history, has been deeply contaminated by the capitalist, "economic" culture. They do not know how to accept sterility, death, failure. They do not wish to recognize their impotence against a culture, and they propose an impossible way out: reject the culture in order to take refuge in a culture of the past. They have lost the secret of making sterility fecund and bringing life out of death through faith, humility, poverty, and hope. The accents of tragic and desperate presumption, the claim to know "how to work things out" which implies the conviction that power is in our hands, fatally provokes the nihilist reaction of artists and young people. The drug culture is the logical response to a movement that appears effective but conceals an actual impotence. But a decision that is lucidly reasoned, intelligent and, above all, coherent is still capable of arousing admiration, enthusiasm and decision.

The only answer that can help our culture—a culture that looks heroic but is in fact mean-spirited, that seems to carry action to the outer limits of endurance but is in fact lazy, that sounds lucid but is in fact disoriented—is to let itself die.

Religion is powerless to promote a clear-eyed commitment because it has moved away from the radicalism of the gospel and is proposing an apparent renewal, with moralistic and Philistine variations. Political considerations control and stifle attempts at real renewal, which degenerate into quantitative programs that defer piously to the centers of power. We are in the desert of sterility, and only when we come to recognize this will we be able to hope for fruitfulness.

The desert of Luke is not the sand-and-rock desert of the prophets. It is the sterile womb of a woman from which no life emerges. It is very similar to our own desert, which is empty of all that is human; it is the loneliness of the person, noncommunication; and for this reason it is anti-eucharistic. The person who is not received, not accepted, is a person incapable of giving thanks. We can only be grateful for *living*, and not for what we have and what can be taken away. "The man who lives will praise you, Lord." We can give thanks only for that which is permanent, which lasts, and which therefore is immune to the fear of corrosion, destruction, and loss; and that is simply to be rooted in the earth, in existence. Those who are not received, and are therefore excommunicated, search for reasons outside of themselves to love life. They look for them outside and beyond life, and their "thanks" are illusory.

This is the hour for prophets, the urgent hour for recognizing and forcefully denouncing the sterility of the world. If industrial society will accept its failure and death, it will be saved. It will be saved "through fire," as Paul says. It is urgent that economic persons, the super-producers, should see clearly that there is no difference between them and young drug addicts. All are in the desert of sterility. The drug addicts know it. It is urgent that the matron who is self-satisfied because she zealously devotes herself to works of charity should discover herself to be very close to the woman who accepts being a sex object and follows her destiny. The two of them are in the desert, with the difference that the sex object can notice the daily depreciation of her value in the consumer market. Only an awareness of sterility can save us. *Homo oeconomicus* continues to produce, invent, and perfect many things, but not the person.

2

The Enemy

Jesus, full of the Holy Spirit, then returned from the Jordan and was conducted by the Spirit into the desert for forty days, where he was tempted by the devil. During that time he ate nothing, and at the end of it he was hungry.

The devil said to him, "If you are the Son of God, command this stone to turn into bread."

Jesus answered him, "Scripture has it, 'not on bread alone shall a man live.' "

Then the devil took him up higher and showed him all the kingdoms of the world in a single instant. He said to him, "I will give you all this power and the glory of these kingdoms; the power has been given to me and I will give it to whomever I wish. Prostrate yourself in homage before me, and it shall all be yours."

In reply, Jesus said to him, "Scripture has it, 'You shall do homage to the Lord your God; him alone shall you adore!' "

Then the devil led him to Jerusalem, set him on the parapet of the temple, and said to him, "If you are the Son of God, throw yourself down from here, for Scripture has it, 'He will bid his angels watch over you'; and again, 'With their hands they will support you, that you may never stumble on a stone.' "

Jesus said to him in reply, "It also says, 'You shall not put the Lord your God to the test.' "

When the devil had finished all the tempting he left him, to await another opportunity (Lk 4,1–13).

Like everyone else, the Son of Man has to make a decision. The temptations of the desert schematize the three lines that constitute our existence: *possession–power–worth.* "Command this stone to be turned into bread." "I will give you all this power and the glory of these kingdoms." "If you are the Son of God, throw yourself down from here." The whole history of the person is articulated around these three passions, and they are the warp and woof of our interpersonal encounters. We recognize this schema of the person through its deformities: avarice, tyranny, vanity. Apparently there is no other destiny for us than to live out these forms of our existence in a disturbed and abnormal way.

The dynamic of liberation is inspired and put into action by the search for a wholesome and peaceful exercise of these human values. A person without possession, power, and worth is not a person. The study of natural law is oriented by an intuition for the structural importance of these three elements. In law it is very difficult to discover possession, power, or worth in a pure state. Natural law has not totally freed itself from certain cultural forms in which it is understood that the person has achieved a certain balance of justice.

The temptation of the static conception of life is found in this effort to come up with the mythical person in whom the three structural elements are supposed to have arrived at perfection, or the attempt to construct a historical person to serve as a model for future generations as one having reached a relative perfection. History is the history of liberation, the constant search for this balance. Revolutionary movements come and go with the intent of demolishing the crystallizations that the conservative forces defend. History consists in smashing these schemata to protect us from ourselves, so that we will search valiantly for our true humanization. To sum up: we are tempted to absolutize the Sabbath and to die defending it, and the leaders of history are precisely those who destroy the Sabbath in order to liberate us. Our history, always new, will have this rhythm: remake the Sabbath—destroy the Sabbath; imprison us in the Sabbath—free us from the Sabbath.

The itinerary of Jesus presented as the ideal person passes through this test. It is important to stress the form of sacred drama that the gospel gives to this primordial choice. The Holy

Spirit and Satan, light and darkness. The essential structure of the person remains ambiguous, because evil creeps into both the commitment to defend the person and the commitment to defend structural law. We will never be able to affirm that good is totally on one side and evil totally on the other.

When it is said: "Property is theft," a historical and cultural form of property is under attack, and the arrow is well aimed. A squadron is mobilized, armed with dynamite and bulldozers, which inflicts a demolishing blow on the juridical absolutism of property. Nevertheless, the statement is metaphysically untrue: The person is property and the person is possession. The mistake arises from the confusion between what is historical and what is metaphysical, the phenomenological and the dialectic.

Here in Latin America a culturalist Christianity feeds conservative movements that have different names in different countries and are the most evident proof of this confusion. The most "cynical" of these is the Tradition-Family-Property movement. The pillar upholding this trilogy is, of course, property. The movement is widespread among the upper classes, who are good at defending their vested interests, and is looked upon benignly by many among the hierarchy who fear change of any sort. Raising the standard of family, tradition, and property is like raising the cross of Christ to defend petty ideas and using religion because of its influence over the people.

The option they present is this: Either you accept things as they are or you will witness the total destruction of society, the family, and the person. Naturally, this propaganda takes on all the emotional and sentimental tonalities designed to impress the people. It plays, at the people's level of understanding, upon the enormous ambiguity of values that indeed have a great fascination and an undeniable dignity. The person is defined as possession, power, and worth. Therefore you should respect the property of those who have it; the authority of those in power; the prestige of those who, because of their blood-lines, race, or culture, are superior to the rest. Flattering popular demand, apparently respecting tradition, they manage to tighten the chains, forcing the people to accept their lot without hope and in practice ruling out all possibility of progress.

People of the gospel find themselves between the Spirit and Satan; their option runs along these three lines, and it *is* an option, not an inheritance. I am a person; therefore I am possession, power, and worth. I am a person, and therefore I must realize myself through possession, power, and worth. I must realize myself, starting not from zero but from a position of alienation, and my option will necessarily have the stamp of liberation. The new person is born in the process of liberation. Since we will have the opportunity to come back to the matter of possession, we are interested now in reflecting a bit on power and worth.

Power is the center of the person, it is identified with our relationships with other people and with things. It is a decision through which human relationships enter into history. Power has come to have for us a pejorative meaning; it signifies a relationship of master-servant, exploiter-exploited, a vertical relationship of dominion and slavery. In every relationship of power there immediately comes about a relationship of superior to inferior which in turn begets rivalry. From the primitive forms of genital potency to the higher forms of politics, art, and science, our discovery of our power is accompanied by our dream of superiority over the other. Power is the natural escape from all frustration, the refuge from fear, the compensation for not being of worth. Power is like a bridge uniting possession and worth, and it suffers repercussions as a consequence. The desire of the person to become powerful generates anguish and insecurity and is the cause of the oppression of others. Power, in the historical order in which we live, is altered by three factors: insecurity, fear, and ignorance of the other.

Power plays upon the deepest need of every person, the need to be accepted. This is our real problem, which is the problem of love. The delightful heroine of *Our Town* by Thornton Wilder is an adolescent girl who is continually asking her mother if she, the girl, is beautiful, if she can be pleasing to others, if she can be accepted. The psychic problem of adolescence is that of being accepted: For the boy it is the question of his strength and genital power, for the girl the question of beauty. This need, which has a built-in insecurity since it is at the mercy of time, is deeply wounded along the way through inhibitions, negative experiences, and competition. We gravitate toward power to the degree of our insecurity; that is, we bank more on the possibility of imposing ourself, of forcing acceptance of ourself from others, than on the quiet acceptance that must come from ourself through the inner strength of our person. Were it not for this insecurity, this need to interject a non-self so that the self might be accepted, our relationships would not be so full of drama.

The fields that offer us the possibility of creating spheres of power, that produce the "uniform" needed in order to be accepted by others, are the political, the religious, and the economic spheres.

In itself politics ought to be a coordination of people and purposes to bring about the material welfare of the group. But people have to get elected, and because of their fear of not being *accepted* their insecurity becomes tyranny and violence. They produce between themselves and others a gap that becomes increasingly wider and foggier—the gap created by ideology. Ideology gives people power and separates them more and more from what is human. There is a kind of parallel in advertising that disguises the product it sells and becomes more expensive and more imposing than the product itself. Enormous neon signs, four or five stories high—and the pills they are selling are hardly to be seen. One needs a disguise to exercise power over others.

A primitive human community will accept the tyrant only if it is intimidated by threats or dazzled by the trappings of power. As I write, I am thinking of Pedro Antonio, the chief of the Ye'cuana tribe in the Amazon jungle; naked except for a simple piece of red cloth wrapped around his middle, he imposes his powerful personality on the tribe without shouts, without weapons, and with very few words. I'd ask myself, Who are the primitives? We, who need so many threats and signs of power? Or these muscular people whose tremendous tolerance for pain reminds us of the Spartans, and who maintain perfect order, a steady rhythm of work, and a bond of unity among them with only the leadership of this unthreatening man who, dressed in his *guayuro* like all the rest, looks out on them serenely from his hammock?

As the human community advances and grows in awareness, the power of individuals comes into conflict with the power of tyrants. And the latter, to defend themselves, must become more astute, more intelligent, more suave in appearance and tougher in reality.   In one epoch people like Kant and Hume, in signing their letters, called themselves 'most humble servants,' making obeisance to the throne and the altar. Today they are on familiar terms with chiefs of state and defer, in everything having to do with artistic criteria, to the judgment of their illiterate chiefs. Tyrants can no longer count on a display of their power of repression and punishment nor on the symbols of their personal prestige; they must control all the roads along which their subjects might rise up and strip their power from them. "The master no longer says: You must think as I do or die. He says: You are free not to think as I do, you will keep your life, property, everything; but from this moment on you will be an intruder among us" (M. Horkeimer and T. Adorno, *Dialéctica del iluminismo*, p. 161).

In order to stay in power and neutralize all attempts to subvert it a system has been constructed, so clever that today it is impossible to recognize in political power a means for helping people to coordinate their efforts in the search for their material well-being. It is a tragic circle: the more our awareness of people grows, the more powerful and irrational political power becomes. We are afraid of people. Political power is employing more than ninety percent of its energies, economic resources, time, and other means at its disposal to planning and organizing methods of defense and aggression, leaving less than a wretched ten percent for the development of the city. In Third World countries one can see at a glance what is happening in a more embryonic form in other countries. There is a clear division of powers: cultural, economic, and political power are all in different hands and not under the control of one individual. Political power cannot be strength, the wisdom of the government, the interpretation of what we want and where we want to go; it is nothing more than a system of defense and of controls in order to give an open field to those who hold economic power. Political power is the keeper of order, the bodyguard for whoever manages the economy; it is aware of everything except that the economy itself is the life blood of the political community. Can you trust the good will, the religious sense, the "Christian formation" of a ruler who takes on the exercise of power in this structure?

Politics will find its strength and value within and of itself if it obtains a consensus on a program of decisions and projects that are designed to liberate the oppressed classes, that is, designed to cure social evils. If it is true that we do not start from zero but from an alienated and sick society, then every political action should be both creative and constructive; it should heal and liberate. As a logical consequence the centers of creative and constructive action ought to be where social evils, the source of alienation, are most visible and easiest to correct. In the long run coercion, punishment, and political prisons would become unnecessary because all would be in agreement on this program for human development.

But where political activity has to protect the plundering and robbery of foreigners who come to take bread from the children of the land, politics becomes power, that is, it substitutes for a vacuum. And this vacuum can be filled only with repressive violence and arid symbols. It is normal that violent people, not "good" people, are the ones who accept responsibility for these structures. To govern, to accept responsibility, is the highest function that we can exercise; it is the noblest and most exhausting office. But within the capitalist-imperialist structure, which does not respect geographical limits or cultural traditions or local economies, heads of state cannot be "good" people, people of "good will"; even less can they be Christian. Indeed, they are not serving others, the social body, but money, power, the absentee master: "I will give you all this power and the glory of these kingdoms; . . . prostrate

yourself in homage before me." "Him alone shall you adore."
The only Christian alternative open to political leaders would
be to effectively deny this dependence, putting into action a
constructive and liberating kind of politics and being ready to
die for it.

There is a superficial and formal kind of moralism that
would like to justify and honor those who accept the burden
and responsibility of a difficult moment in history because
they "do the best they can"; because "you can't doubt their
good intentions." Religious leaders put a halo around the
heads of political leaders that can distort the judgment of the
people. But the fact of the matter is that either political power is
a service for the liberation of the oppressed or it is tyranny.
Either it is the highest expression of concern for others or it is
an expression of fierce and aggressive egoism. And all political
acts that might seem good, prudent, and wise are vitiated to
the core by this option. One cannot identify politics with the
liberation of the oppressed when it has for its program the
increase of the economic power of nations and vested interest,
a program which, instead of lifting up the oppressed, is designed to fill the coffers of capitalist enterprises.

In Medellín, the Latin American bishops saw this in a moment of clarity. But why, after that, do they go on classifying as
"good" and "well-intentioned" those who control unjust
structures which they do nothing to change, but on the contrary defend with imprisonment and torture? This kind of
political power is intrinsically anti-Christian and contrary to
the gospel. There is no political vision possible for the Christian other than that of giving food to the hungry, clothes to the
naked, a house to the homeless. In political terms this means
to make decisions not with a view to making money but to
liberating the oppressed.

The gospel is resoundingly opposed to religious power but
deeply respects the method of the Father, the plan that God
has followed in his relationship with us: Form a people, guide
them through their history, reveal himself to them as goodness, providence, salvation, retribution, and resurrection.
Thus the people would be able to say, in the ups-and-downs of

their history: "God is with us," he has not abandoned us; "he is our God and we are his people." This people has a political structure, a visible body which Christ came not to suppress but to bring to perfection. The church, as the successor of this covenant people, has its structure, its visibility; it lives side by side with the political society and within the political society. The church's purpose is that history, what we all live through—workers, artists, businesspeople, all of us—shall become the history of salvation, of justice, of communion: that a history full of despair shall become eucharistic history.

The redemptive force of religion becomes religious power at the very moment when the one responsible for passing the dynamic force of salvation on to the world is transformed into the leader of a religious group that he feels he must govern, organize, and structure. Then it is not a group of human beings in search of salvation for themselves and others, but rather a well-established club with its statutes, laws, and political structure. The one in power shapes the group in his own image, and then the group demands that he exercise power in a determined way. The First Epistle of Peter defines the tone of authority in the church in a graphic way: "God's flock is in your midst; give it a shepherd's care. Watch over it willingly as God would have you do, not under constraint; and not for shameful profit either, but generously. Be examples to the flock, not lording it over those assigned to you" (1 Pt 5,2–3).

The church is a prophetic gathering in search of a liberation that is given, a justice that must be established, and a communication that must be brought into being. It lives among a desperate humanity which has come to the desert and has to be made into eucharist—that is, happy in its existence because it is loved, because it is orientated by a hope that is identical with the Paschal hope.

The religious structure becomes a power structure when it enters into the mainstream of economics—accumulating, distributing, and consuming—and withdraws from what belongs to it specifically—creating, discovering, searching. It is true that Christ left the church goods and values to be guarded and transmitted, goods which are in essence the Word and Life, intimate forces of transformation. Nevertheless the responsibility for this transmission demands a search, not a tactical search with the object of making this wealth acceptable, but a search for the forms of salvation: for the moments of liberation that this Word itself engenders in history, moments that constitute the occasions, the points of departure, in the successive stages wherein the church is the responsible party. To understand these "forms of salvation" and these successive stages, it is necessary to be within the currents of salvation, not "outside" them and still less "against" them.

Because of this necessity of being within the currents of salvation, the criteria for choosing those who will be entrusted with leadership must be radically changed. A schematic criterion could well be formulated with this question: Should command precede function or should function precede command? It is true that David was the smallest of the sons of Jesse, the most insignificant, the least "functional"; it is true that God chooses things that are useless to confound the strong. But it is also true that historically those who are consecrated as leaders end up being uprooted from the people, from history, from life. And when the uprooting from place, culture, and lifestyle is complete, the leaders are sent to announce the message of liberation whose origin goes back to Christ.

Without a radical change of perspective it is hard to expect people chosen and educated according to this criterion not to opt for the economic line and for power. They will not go down into the ranks to encourage others, to guide them in their search for the way and the direction leading to salvation. Instead, they will see themselves as distributors of consumer values—which of themselves can be quite noble. Unfortunately this approach produces a static group of leaders and turns religious authority into a matter of power. It becomes even more dangerous when analogies to the political system are sought; for religious authority is not, like the political system, subject to criticism and savage power struggles. It does not have the opportunity the political power has of becoming human, of changing, when faced with the necessity of providing, out of very scarce resources, for economic needs that are becoming increasingly pressing and frightening. Confrontation with reality, the need to keep their feet on the ground, endows tyrants with a certain solitary grandeur that is lacking in ecclesiastical leaders. We must recognize how difficult it is to prevent responsibility in a religious community from becoming religious power. It is attracted in many ways to this same political power, which is ready to share, to listen, and even to be obedient as long as its regal rights are respected and it is given credit for righteousness—something only religious power can confer on it.

The Christian community itself seeks the security that comes from power rather than sharing the insecurity, the doubt, the anxious waiting of one who is searching with the others. It is felt that that kind of insecurity is nothing more than confusion, superficiality, immaturity: The role of religious authority is to command in God's name, give cut-and-dried orders spelled out in precise detail.

The "economic" generation begs religious power to rescue it from the desert by some economic means and through a simple kind of mediation which would stimulate the mechanisms of repentance, punishment, and pardon. I was present at a retreat for rich people where, at one point, they all burst into tears like children who had been punished and become repentant. They did not, as far as I know, thereafter change their lifestyle, taking upon themselves and sharing the lot of those "persecuted for holiness' sake." And these rich people go on being the pride and joy of their spiritual directors. To put it bluntly: The Christian community wants to find in the representative of religious power a teacher who will relieve them of the tiring need to search, a judge who will make little of their guilt and fear complexes, dissolving them without difficulty. In other words they are looking for a sorcerer capable of exorcising their terror of the unknown. And we should never forget that in each one of us there is hidden a traumatized and disillusioned person who is seeking power in the easiest way as a matter of compensation. And that is all it takes for the perennially vital force of the gospel to be reduced to religious power which, like all other powers, is unjust and inhuman and gives evidence of impoverishment and vanity.

In this revisionist epoch, religious power is being exposed to behind-doors criticism which is reducing and transforming it to some degree. The number of those who see economic religion as a consumer product is diminishing, and the gospel is being discovered as the content of an integral liberation. The new Christians are increasingly less interested in the person who holds religious power, whereas they receive with open arms anyone who goes out to meet them in the desert where their uncertain search has led them. Soon ecclesiastics will be absent from among the politicians on the reviewing stands and from the dedications of theaters, shopping centers, and gambling casinos. Only "power" has a right to be there with the other powers.

Cultural power is the inevitable consequence of political and economic power. Whoever has power in their hands imposes a culture and excludes as barbaric, as a counter-culture, the customs and traditions that do not meet their standards. In this way there is brought into being the rootless kind of culture characteristic of conquered countries.

Darcy Ribeiro, describing the ethos of Latin American culture, writes in *Cuadernos latinoamericanos:*

First, the conquest provoked the compulsive uprooting of the ethnocentric tribal conceptualizations of the Indian and the black that had allowed them to accept their self-image, seeing in it a model of the human. Later they formed a new concept of themselves which, because it was a projection of the idea that the conquered were becoming increasingly unequal partners in a coalition, was necessarily despicable. For the actual rulers described them as grotesque creatures, intrinsically inferior and incapable of making progress.

Through a kind of historical vengeance, countries that imposed their culture on conquered peoples are now in the throes of an analogous violence. Our "western Christian" culture, which was for centuries identified with human culture, is no longer a true expression of community, a symbol of growth, but rather one of the projections of the economic that the individual is obliged to accept because of external factors such as propaganda and political pressure. The uprooted person is not only the peasant or the highlander, reduced to dire poverty, but also the city dweller. The cultural uprooting, of which youth especially is aware, is a universal phenomenon. We all fall prey to mistaken priorities like the "natives": We buy liquor instead of bread; we have a television set before we have a decent bed; we drug ourselves rather than cope with things. Cultural power dominates us all.

Political power makes use of persons and groups who have a certain artistic bent but are not autonomously creative, enlisting them in the ranks of "cultural power." Tyranny fears the creations of the artist, and so it promotes controlled cultural exhibitions. A dictatorship opens up many avenues for the spread of culture, but it blocks off the road to the artist who is discovering the authentic roots of a culture and revealing the true character of the people. Art is always the discovery of the real power possessed by the universal person, and it is therefore in opposition to all specific powers. Poetry is always the "song of returning." Art always reveals the person as in a state of exile, of nonfreedom; and indeed there is a sense in which it is the exiles' song of their return. Cultural power, on the other hand, is a direct means of drugging the person. It does not explore the profound and the true, but goes along the way of escape.

In Latin America political and cultural power have for centuries hidden the continent's originality. Today the church is here more as a religious power than as a force for religion. If the religious faith of the Latin American people could be measured in terms of colleges, convents, and temples, any medieval Christian would be truly impressed. Political power has undergone various changes, with regimes skillfully alternating; but the norm has not changed. Here culture—an imported product when it originates in art, indeed great art—is transformed into the power culture, because it is alien to the continent, as I discovered on hearing Beethoven's *Sixth* played by a group of *criollos* in the southern part of Venezuela. Latin

America is the continent where colonialism has created between the forces of the land and the structure imposed by a
foreign power a fissure so deep that the alienation now common to all the countries in the world has here become intolerable. It is this which will be the starting point for the reduction
of political power to politics, of religious power to faith, and of
cultural power to artistic contemplation. On other continents
this alienation has come about through corruption, fatigue, or
lack of vigilance; here it has come about through the impotence
of the conquered races.

Today the weak are gaining strength in the cultural area
through a new generation of poets, novelists, and cinematog-
raphers whose works have achieved the status of bestsellers in
the world market. In the political area they are gaining power
through revolutionary movements that are now being
evaluated in the distorted terms of the incumbents—
expropriations, kidnappings, and the like. But in time they
will appear in their true historical dimension, purer in their
gospel inspiration. In the religious sector, a populist spir-
ituality is being created and injected into the roots that the
conquest left so badly mutilated and burned, a piety which is
all the while withdrawing itself from religious power. It is a
continent which, on a massive scale and in a variety of ways, is
rejecting power and searching for a more real relationship
between people.

Power has three roots: distrust, fear, and pride. Power is the
pathological escape from a situation of distrust that begins in
infancy. Contributing to this distrust is the presence in society
of certain cultural models, impersonal or personified, on
which high value is set. The cultural atmosphere keeps them
alive and in their prime; and they all involve prowess
—athletic, sexual, or intellectual. Political dictatorships are
skilled in creating cultural models—carrying the process to the
point of becoming sheer nonsense—to the end of creating the
one and only model of which they will make good use. And
this exaltation of the model readily engenders fear, and the
fearful person will normally take refuge in power. I lived out
my formative years under a fascist dictatorship, and I well

remember the obsession with physical excellence. Our cultural model was to be that of a caste, descendants of gladiators and legionaries. However, through a dialectical contradiction, I was incredibly fascinated by the intellectuals of the opposition, who exalted the value of weakness, goodness, the ideal of going unarmed, of seeing value in ourselves for what we are, and not for what we can do.

Distrust is the point of departure for aggressiveness and the desire to dominate; it sets one aside from the normal path of development that is everyone's destiny.

Power is always a qualitative or quantitative alienation. Because of it I construct for myself a personality that is not mine. I wear a mask, or I take some quality of mine and strain it to an unreal intensity. I become a boxer when I should be a philosopher, or I try to pass for a heavyweight when I am hardly a flyweight. Family ambition, the ridicule of friends, the disgrace that comes to someone who has failed—all these make us lose sight of relationship, of communion, which is the true meaning of existence. Power arrests all growth and breaks into the world with violence and untruth. It puts an end to relationships and stimulates competition; it gives rise to the temptation to destroy everything that threatens the stability of the position we have achieved.

Fear displaces relationship and pride hides the frustration of not having achieved what is essential—communion with the others, liberation from loneliness. And these defeated persons project themselves into alienated structures, they create models to their own image, and the chain reaction continues. Who will bring us back to our authentic selves, rescuing us from our alienation? For us Christians the answer is redemption, rebirth of the kind Jesus talked about to Nicodemus. And the test of someone who has been born of the Spirit from on high is to be open to dialogue and freed from the lure of power. It is necessary that our personal strength, which springs from our being, from faithfulness to our existence, be tested continuously on the level of personal relationship. If we instill *fear* or *veneration,* it means that we are hemmed in by power. "This person is too powerful, dangerous, distant, or old for us to try to dialogue":

If this is the way people feel about us, then it is necessary that we "cover ourselves with ashes," that we do penance, because our person, the center of our person, is truly in danger.

And here we reopen the eternal problem of acceptance: Communion is a movement that goes not from me to others but from others to me. If this movement exists, if I leave the way open, I can free myself from the deformities of power. I cannot do it alone by meditation or making a decision. I must work it out in my relationships.

Through power we can avoid the problem of relationships, building a false relationship apart from persons and against them: a relation that makes persons into things. Rebirth consists in a refashioning of the relationship, in living it deeply with those who oblige us to be what we are, who see us not as we represent ourselves to be, what we think ourselves to be, but what we are. The problem is very difficult—I would say almost insoluble—because even the man-woman relationship, which ought to be the most liberating, the most real, the most true, is generally effected through power. It is compromised in advance by "something in the middle"—by money, position, or by something that can be considered objectively as external to the person and renders the person separate, something that prevents two people from "touching each other in their essence."

Perhaps the day is not too far distant in which we will have a new kind of relationship due to the fact that the two people involved will be able to accept the suffering of time, of poverty, and of renunciation. We should spread the idea that relating is difficult. We should not do this out of masochism or victimism but because the remaking of a person is a long and arduous business. In the nineteenth chapter of Matthew, the Master lays down a definition of the man-woman encounter so difficult that his listeners, not without a bit of irony, are led to comment: "If that is the case between man and wife, it is better not to marry." On this point he alludes to a liberating relation which becomes the ideal point, a kind of utopia possible in human encounter.

The theme of power offers us an occasion to take a look at

this proposal for liberation in human encounter. Celibacy as a condition demanded for entrance into the sacerdotal caste can become twisted into becoming a center for power instead of a cause of poverty and, for that reason, a stripping of the person to the bareness of being. There can be no doubt that power finds its deepest growth in sex. With the power of re-production we become rooted to the earth, we enter in a privileged way into creation. Labor, the economy, politics—all take second place, since they are so much less vital to the person than sexual activity. But even as we become rooted in the earth we make it our own, subject it, dominate it. Through sexual activity life is transmitted, and with life the *pride of dominating* and the *fear of violation*, two coefficients of power.

The fear of freedom, to an even greater extent than it is reflected in political or cultural structures, arises in that inti-mate sphere of the person—sex. Freud was the first to grasp intuitively the connection between sex, civilization, and his-tory; and today it is of the utmost importance that the human quest for understanding should examine this link. Bergman has an artistic intuition about it, and his whole artistic product revolves around this theme: People are unable to arrive at their own roots, unable to establish their identity; there is no real man-woman encounter, and violence is unleashed on the world—an anonymous violence, not identifiable or reachable. Entering directly into sex as components are distrust, fear, and pride; they make of the primal encounter, constitutive of what is human, a form of oppression and violence. There is born the person of power—an obscene mixture, humanly incurable, of distrust, fear, and pride. Chastity, the renunciation of genital sex—is this the way to liberation? Is this the way to help us find our true selves? Could there come out of chastity the ability to love, to establish a relationship that would not make things out of persons? that would not subdue, would not instill fear—and hence would not bring about reactions of violence? It is a question today's youth is asking in the face of a value that has always been taken for granted. It seems to me important that the possibility of this renunciation of genital sex should cease to be exclusively of the church and should be suggested to youth groups not motivated by moralistic or cultural principles. On this search young people would be responding obediently to the intuition that in the very personal, and in itself very personalizing, act of sex there can lie hidden violence and brutality, and that this renunciation of theirs is related to the bringing about of peace.

Surely the ecclesiastical state in general offers us no hope of liberation from power; all we see is a hypocritical disguise of human prepotency. Our generation refuses to believe that God is pleased with suffering; that people can serve God better by not using their sexual powers; that virginity, which the Bible speaks of as a grandeur and a "closeness to God," consists merely in the rejection of an act which is in itself immensely fulfilling. I think that virginity, one of the themes of the New Testament, is synonymous with integrity, non-violation, the worth of the person finally liberated from fear and aggressiveness.

If chastity would really get to this root where the history begins that is translated into the numbers of the tortured, of those dead of hunger and violence, of the poor kept alive with the barest minimum so that they will continue to produce for their masters, I still don't think many would be disposed to accept chastity in the way they are disposed to give their lives to bring peace to people. But if chastity is a "privilege," a factor of power—humiliation that turns into pride, poverty that becomes wealth, loneliness consoled by adulation—then chastity cannot be a value. Because of the trust I have in Christ and in his words, because of the radiant examples I have seen here and there in certain persons, I think that this foregoing of genital sex is a lowly, painful, and dramatic sign of how this "power" can be attacked at the root.

Three questions still remain to be asked: Is this the only way to liberation? What meaning and tonality can this search have? What is the relation between chastity and the drama of the world? If you tell me from a "spiritual" eminence that chastity has only one meaning—that of glorifying God—I will answer that the glory of God cannot have any other meaning than a step toward justice, toward communion, toward the humanization of human relations, toward the things wherein our true happiness lies. In the discourse of the Last Supper Jesus identifies his Father's glory with unity among those who believe in him.

It cannot be affirmed that choosing to renounce the use of sex is the only road to liberation from power. But it is the "sign," the going down to the deepest level wherein resides the creativity of the person, our identity, the root of our being and existence. It is the anticipation of all that people long for when they wistfully express a hope for peace.

The man-woman encounter is then no longer a sign of the transmission and multiplication of life, but a sign of the search for life, a sign that love can exist apart from power. Only those who "understand the mystery" of the word directed personally to them can follow this road. And they must live out this mystery in darkness as a diminution, an impoverishment, an emptiness, a humbling. This sense of the uselessness, of the anti-triumphalism, of chastity is not accidental; it is at the heart of renunciation. When a "consecrated" person tells me that chastity has no meaning, all I can do is point out the alternatives—either chastity-power and therefore non-chastity, or chastity-humbling, impoverishment, emptiness. There is no in-between.

We can find something similar only in people who spend their whole lives in political prisons or in exile, putting up with the limitation of their freedom for the sake of freedom. If we reflect on history, we will often see that what makes certain values come to the fore is their apparent denial. No one has been more in favor of freedom than someone who has renounced freedom. No one does more of a favor to the triumph of an idea than someone who tries to stamp it out by the most violent means.

It is not a choice that is easily made through thought and reflection. Events bring it about and, in the case of the celibate, it is a mysterious call stronger than any arising from historic violence and ideology. The risk is great because one must walk a very narrow path between two abysses: on one side the abyss of power; on the other that of necrophilia, that is, of despairing. Prisoners who are victims of violence can fall into this same temptation, asking themselves, "What good is all this? There will always be servants and masters, exploited and exploiting; future generations cannot certainly be any happier than this one." Those who suffer the violence of God should fill the earth with hope; they should be able to walk the narrow path between their temptations, holding on strongly to their faith in the coming of the new person; they should learn to be still in order to discover in their senseless renunciation (like someone imprisoned in a concentration camp because of fidelity to an ideal) faith in people, in their being reborn from on high, in their making progress toward justice, fraternity, dialogue.

If chastity slips into the temptation of wanting to be a "sign," of becoming a model, and if one seeks to be admired, accepted as a superior being, chastity has no value toward liberation. I have a gut feeling that in chastity you have a résumé of all the renunciations, all the impoverishments, all the humiliations of human beings. It is enough for me to think about the poor who are not accepted, not loved, not prized, about the obstinate idealists who lay down their lives for a dream, in order to feel that God has considered me in the deep root of all that is human, in the hidden depths whence originate freedom and power, fellowship and communion, or exploitation and, therefore, peace and war. God has thrust me into all this as negation, as emptiness, there where all human humiliations and impoverishments occur, there where the center of the drama is and where I suspect the center of liberation is to be found.

I can't tell by what mysterious law renunciation can contribute to a solution or how emptiness can bring about fullness or how a non-relationship can correct and transform a relationship. I know that the path of history is a sad Exodus. And there are—to paraphrase the gospel discourse on chastity—those who are beaten down by the violence of others, unconscious victims of the exercise of power. And there are those who suffer violence with a greater awareness and by their clamorous protests give hope and release and irrepressible force of rejection that calls forth the explosions of liberty and the splendid hours of history. When renunciation does not come from a low motive, it becomes an act of courage, it is a daring exploration into the human. If Christ had never existed, if there had never been those who come back from this exploration more truly human, it would not be right even to attempt the venture. Whether it is successful or not, the one who lives this renunciation cannot say. Only the "others" can say if they have finally discovered the very rare case of someone who knows how to love without "thingifying," who has not lost any of the nuances of human tenderness, someone who is capable of re-creating, of helping to stand again, a person stricken with the anemia of lovelessness.

It is not altogether a bad thing that celibacy is a non-value today, that it should be not only looked down upon but even devalued within the ecclesial structure itself. It can be accepted only as emptiness, humiliation, impoverishment. Only in this way is it a denial of power. Only in this way, stripped of its cultural mystique and the aggressive rhetoric that has been used in its defense, can it be understood by whoever, living within history, is torn by its contradictions.

There is a fascinating episode in the gospel which highlights the vigorous and virile personality of Christ. At the dramatic moment when the Prophet was having a discussion with his adversaries, his family came looking for him, and those inside the house said to him: "Your mother and your brothers are standing outside, and they wish to see you." He answered: "Who is my mother and who are my brothers?" And looking at those who were sitting around him, he said: "These are my mother and my brothers. Whoever does the will of God is brother and sister and mother to me" (Mk 3,31). Indeed, it seems contradictory to seek loneliness when all the while we are trying to solve the problem of communication, to reject love when it is precisely the lack of love that fills our history with sorrow. But we are talking about a loneliness that is orientated toward a fuller insertion in the universe, a renunciation with a view to a more intimate sharing in it. Those who have accepted the mysterious invitation—the ultimate madness—are aware of this.

The gospel leads us to discover the new person in the desert; it is there that the path begins. The new persons accept the desert; they do not take the easy way out to allay their hunger. Nor do they seek any facile way to resolve the problem of loneliness, or their deepest and most vital problem—their identity. Taking a last look at the sacred drama that Mark and Luke have mounted in order to give us a picture of the Messiah as he is, I am struck by how moving the scene is. It reveals the human aspiration to objectify our options and to see them in proper perspective. However, under the attrition of daily life, with the inexorable passage of time, courage wanes. We would like to meet one great test against an adversary of stature, to be challenged to a contest with neat contours that would concentrate all the force of our will. But our history is different: The option is made and renewed under such poor circumstances and with so opaque a vision that at times I ask myself if life is not just too big a challenge.

The gospel attempts to implant in us three ideas for the orientation of our options: *vigilance, poverty,* and *infancy.* The gospel ideal is not the destruction of us, our crucifixion; rather it is new life for us, rejuvenation, rebirth; but to have the courage to be reborn we must keep our outlook and our tastes simple. We must become used to living within our limitations, being comfortable with them—and all the while dreaming a grandiose dream that transcends our capabilities. If this dream had our self as its center, this provisional acceptance of our littleness would be the most deceitful snare of power; but it has as its center the "others," history, human liberation. To maintain this strange balance between poverty and greatness, to be aware of the limitations of the person, and at the same time of the hope that reaches out to the infinity of the Parousia, what else is there to do but live immersed in the meanness of daily living and feel it seep through every pore, accepting it as our lot and combining it with an immense and obscure hope? We all experience great moments in life, and they are not necessarily moments of triumph. They are the moments of deep penetration into the self, of the repose of the self in the essential: the moment of vision, of the profound savor of life. These are the experiences that accompany us in the long march through the colorless and horizonless desert. Despite the parching heat, the poor are able to continue on the march. They would seem to be without hope; yet they smile at life—and you can't smile without hope. We are used to seeing them as fatalists, meekly accepting their lot, because in their journeying they are animated by a hope that is invisible. But the hope hidden within them is so strong that it breaks into joyful song when, surprisingly, the silence is pierced by the sound of a friendly voice. The journey ends in an impromptu way with the lighting of a fire. For this reason theirs is the kingdom of heaven.

3

The Person Alone

You fool! This very night your life shall be required of you. To whom will all this piled-up wealth of yours go? (Lk 12,20)

The whole subject of economics is highly important because it takes in the process of the arrival on the scene and the growth of the person. Although we cannot establish a correspondence between the Marxist idea of economics as the sole determining factor in human conduct on the one hand and the gospel on the other, it is undeniable that Marxist literature has helped us to discover implications in the reading of the gospel that had previously escaped us.

Frightened capitalists, locked up in contemplation of themselves and of things, have become lost in their terrifying solitude through not knowing how to relate to economic goods in a wholesome way. They are people shaped by fear. That great fear that comes to us arises in us from our structure, which is conditioned by time and space. Our drama begins at the very moment when, emerging from our mother's womb, we begin to live in the time and space that is ours. It is then that the alternative of rejecting or accepting is initiated: We feel ourselves drawn to space and time; we are aware of an invitation to rush ahead, and at the same time we are tormented by a longing to be enfolded, to be dependent, to be cared for—the longing to return to the womb.

It is becoming increasingly more important—it is a marginal

note that enriches the dimension of love, so essential to the gospel—that this moment of rupture from life under the control of the mother and the acceptance of life now under our own control be brought about in an atmosphere of warmth and welcome. It is now seen to be more urgent to worry about the psychic health of the child, better to let the child who comes into time and space be with the mother and feel the assuring warmth of her body. Not feeling alone is better than being isolated in an aseptic environment so that another unit of the human race will be germ-free and capable of growing into a beautiful body without kinks or distortions. For example, the child born in the Amazon valley and leaving an Indian mother's womb to enter into space and time is very probably less scarred and conditioned by traumas than a child born in a highly immunized nursery from whence all sickness and death have been expelled, but not fear.

The loving acceptance of time and space can come about only through the discovery of the other and of the others. The presence of people who love one another can make an unpleasant space fascinating and time full of meaning. When I arrived in a place in northeastern Argentina where I was to spend a few years, everything there seemed squalid and hopeless. Time ticked on implacably in that horizonless plain where ghostly trees with sharp-pointed leaves grew, seeming to repel anyone who would venture into the mountain. In time I began to discover that spring also came to the plain—a wild spring, smuggled in, rich in absolutely indescribable colors and perfumes. It was the birth of friendship with the people of the place that made the landscape charming and brought deep meaning to my living with persons who have become bound to my life profoundly and forever.

In trying to affirm ourselves we forget that time and space are internal affairs of the person and apart from us are emptinesses. To occupy more and more space without filling it with friendship, without filling it with humanity, is to sink more and more into isolation. To fill time with things, leaving it empty of "relationships," is to be condemned to anguish. We all discover that time as filled up as ours is becomes anguish at the moment we feel there is not enough of it. Time that appears to be wasted but is blessed with a profound relationship seems rich in meaning. In the end, love is the only thing that fills emptiness, the only reality.

The image of the rich man is instructive: He is alone, firmly set in his frozen self for fear of time and space. Suspended in this terrifying emptiness of time and space, he tries to save himself. If the enterprising people who see themselves as quite productive could realize that the motivation of their activity is nothing more than fear, perhaps they would feel humbled. If we were to see ourselves as insignificant and poor, we would realize what is behind our performance, what are really our motives. It would seem better not to see, to continue living with the little bit of courage that comes from the illusion of doing worthwhile things.

If we were to perceive the ultimate meaning of things—that a kiss can be an act of hatred, that to work can make less sense than the activities of an insane asylum—we would lack the courage to go on living. Nevertheless the alternative is: either time has a creative and constructive meaning for the person, and therefore I must have a greater awareness of what I am and of how much I do; or it is a great spinning about in emptiness, and therefore it is better to do away with one's life.

Instead of exorcising his fear, the rich man lets it become more acute, emptying space and time. If we are locked up in ourselves, blocked off to the point where our self is the center, we can free ourselves only by discovering the other and the others. I want to underline a point here—I will have occasion to develop it later on; it is the answer to a question we ask ourselves continually: "From what does Christ save us; what is salvation, redemption, liberation?" The question is vital, and it can also be formulated another way: "What is being a Christian all about?" Christ rescued us from this loneliness, this being locked up, frozen in the self, and gave us the ability to discover and to communicate with the Other. This is the *one thing that we are radically and incurably unable to do by ourselves.*

In the situation of the rich man, time and space—categories of existence—become absolute values. He tries to fill them with security, so that his self will be protected. He accepts them as the "emptiness of the human" and tries to retrieve them and fill them with security so that he will not feel threatened by them. But the self has no other protection than to give of self, to lose the self—a decision that requires an act of courage, of firm breaking away, the conquest of the fear of dying. Can everybody do this? Are we not so conditioned that it seems impossible in practice? It is at this very point that we encounter the mystery of salvation and redemption. The reason why some are liberated and others are not—and end up in therapy or suicide, or take refuge in power and other forms of cruelty, of "vengeance upon the other"—is a mystery that is beyond us.

If a flower is pleasing to me, I can cut it, accepting the law of time which will make it wither and die, or I can toss its seed into the earth and have it live on continuously. The rich man of Luke's chapter 12 opts for *conservation. He has many things stored away for many years.* Relax, eat heartily, drink well. Enjoy yourself. He is seen to be alone. He reasons with himself because in fact his attitude about goods, his seeing them as things to be stored away rather than vehicles for relationship, reveals him to be a man mired in a state of masturbation, finding in his own body a thing in itself and not a means of relationship. Our decisions are the true picture of our profoundest self.

If our actions are a projection of our self, as in the account of Luke, "masturbation" is disguised by the decision to get rid of fear. "You have many things stored away for many years." A great outpouring of energy intended for the preservation of the self; a sterile circle: contemplation of the body is replaced by narcissistic contemplation of one's own ability and power. The initiatives, the goods, the things that in themselves are oriented toward filling the space and the time of the "human," are instead directed toward protecting the emptiness of time and space so that in this emptiness the solitary self can exist, contemplate itself, and prolong its existence.

If through an instantaneous miracle we could become "real," how quickly would our appraisal of the generation gap change. How much more infantile, less mature, and therefore more pathological, than the young generation would the older generation seem to us in the defense of its turf (Eastern Asia, South Africa, the Middle East, Latin America). This young generation spurns what it has inherited and is breaking away from its dependence on a culture that is "thingified" and "thingifying." Wisdom is not on the side of the father who, to defend his space and time—he says they belong to the son, but in fact they are *his* time and *his* space—does not hesitate to sacrifice his son on the altar of war, a decision that unmasks him. If the time and space really belonged to the son, the father would be willing to lose everything except his son. We can understand this madness only if we realize that they are mad—apparently able to plan for the future but in reality locked up in a pathological egoism.

According to the gospel, the destiny of the "rich" man, the man who has not arrived at the point of discovering the Other, is to be unable to fill space and time with "humanity." For this reason the rich man is always outside history; and although he gives the impression of thinking in concrete terms, of having his feet on the ground, in reality he is more in the abstract than any theorist. For him time is something "out there" and therefore, not being in history, is not creative. His enormous activity is not creative.

In political society, anti-historicity becomes political oppression, and all its efforts are directed to increasing production and distribution, with no concern for human growth and maturation. In the sphere of religion, anti-historicity has the aspect of a moral rigorism that does not have the growth in awareness and liberation of the person as its objective. In short, people who have responsibility create or hold on to instruments of repression (and to hold on to them they must use them), with fatal results.

It does seem as if John Doe, president of a capitalist nation, or Mr. Whatshisname on the board of directors of a huge corporation, or Bishop So-and-so should be capable of taking one step forward; it does seem that with a little good will they could advert to the existence of the others and to the fact that

time is the history of their maturation, of their growth, of their
becoming persons; and that space ought to be occupied by
their real growth. But the truth is that they cannot, any more
than a blind person can go out to look at the almond trees in
bloom. It is hard to admit, nevertheless, that we are asking
these people who are cemented in their infantile history, who
are incapable of distracting their gaze from their own excrement, to see the other. All the decisions they make, even those
apparently for the others—"altruistic"—are actually made in
defense of time and space. Not the time and space of the rest,
which constitute the meaning of history, but time and space
seen as "frightening emptinesses" which must therefore be
filled up with security. But only when time and space are filled
up with "humanity" interiorized in us, do they cease to be
frightening. The apparent creativity of the rich man is, in fact,
nothing more than demolition: "I will pull down my grain bins
and build larger ones."

The conservative, static attitude and the futurist attitude are
projections of the psychic stages of the person. At first sight
this discovery scares us. Political decisions are not made because an eloquent ambassador has persuaded the president to
act in a certain way: the president cannot act in a mature way if
at heart he is still a child. He needs redemption. And I believe
this redemption must descend to our very depths where our
person has become trapped and immobilized. The sign that
redemption has come, that the Savior has reached us in those
depths, is our state of maturity, a capacity for true otherness.
"There was a time when you were darkness, but now you are
light in the Lord. Well, then, live as children of light. Light
produces every kind of goodness and justice and truth. Be
correct in your judgment of what pleases the Lord. Take no
part in deeds done in darkness; rather, condemn them" (Eph
5,8–11).

It has been said over and over again to the point of exaggera-
tion that Christ has liberated us in the realm of the spiritual and
that redemption is an invisible process, that grace leaves us
with our traumas, tics, the structural defects we have that
shape our total physiognomy. In the next life this man will

have a splendid countenance, this girl will have a Botticelli head of hair, that crippled woman will have straight legs. And we must grope in the dark believing that, in that dark, redemption is taking place despite the apparent immobility of our being and the impression that nothing is really happening.

Nevertheless, the description of salvation given us by the New Testament is opposed to this "invisibilist" and "spiritualist" approach. It speaks of a new perspective, a new sensitivity, a radical change of choices and objectives. There is a transformation of the essential even when signs of our past and features of our human physiognomy remain. The change should be especially evident along the lines of otherness, in our ability to make room for the other. The liberation of "sinners," of those cemented in themselves, locked up in their own selves, is to acquire the ability to make room for the other.

It is very difficult to determine whether a person is liberated or not. When psychoanalysis becomes purely technical, it will be able to render a valuable service. But in any event, what is the use of knowing one is locked up in oneself, or is in the anal stage, if one cannot get free? We have no doubt but that the ones who are in this stage are the first to stockpile arms, open military bases, protect the stock market and the banks; and that with military and economic power they will always defend their space, investing with spurious splendor their sad, infantile history.

Apparent altruism and the magnanimous gesture can be just as deceptive as the familiar selfless and overprotective mother and the gruff, hearty big daddy. Seemingly they are altruistic persons, dedicated to the welfare of their children, but in fact they are incapable of genuine otherness. Their devouring egoism, to feel alive, must be fed by others. Their love does not respect the right of the other to grow. They are in a constant state of dependence which at heart is nothing more than a reflection of the present state of someone who is forever in chains. In the familiar song of love of First Corinthians we discovered the paradox that not every kind of self-giving is love: "If I give everything I have to feed the poor and hand over my body to be burned, but have not love, I gain nothing"

(1 Cor 13,3). How I would like to write the following questions on the walls of many homes, convents, and welfare offices: "Are you sure, you who are giving your life, who are delivering up your body to be burned for others, are you sure that you really love? Have you discovered the other and the others? Or are the people around you nothing more than a context in which you can live alone without being bothered?"

"The others" are the sign—if they can grow in my environs, if they feel free, if they find that my love and friendship are liberating. The sign is also my condition of loneliness. Pasolini has sensed this human mystery and has touched on it in his *Teorema*. The gift of self to the other is not enough to free certain persons from their inner loneliness; loneliness is not a temporal or spatial category, it is a psychological state. Loneliness remains with us and in us even when our situation is rich in options with respect to places, persons, and things. *Can one person free another from loneliness? Can woman free man and the man free woman from their loneliness?* It would seem so because in the latter case love is present, the love of friendship, the kind of love that exhausts the full possibilities of sex. But experience has taught me the contrary; now I believe that in itself the man-woman encounter is not liberating. True, love in itself is liberating, but the possibility always exists of a "beyond," a "before," a "much deeper."

The capacity to love, to discover the other, is already a sign of essential wholesomeness, of liberation achieved. It is true that liberation is progressive and evolves in time and space in the very history of the encounter. Nevertheless man cannot give to man, nor man to woman, this liberation. Love is liberating when it is truly love, discovery of the other, "otherness"; but this love is found in someone already liberated, who is therefore capable of discovering the other.

There are people whom no one can free from the tragic blocking of their own selves, of their narcissistic fixation —people who are incapable of love. They are forever attributing their failure at love to other people and to events. Their complaints about circumstances reveal that they have never learned how to get beyond the infantile stage. I believe that only the Redeemer can free them from this ontological loneliness, which has to be a kind of hell. For this reason Jesus does not come through to me as the "ornament" or the "glory" of humankind or as a name to be written on the bronze tablets of a nation or a city. No, were it not for the Redeemer, there would be no hope for us; for although we can do practically anything and are almost omnipotent, we do not achieve the one thing on which all history depends—*to see, to recognize, and to love the other*. We can dwell in stellar space, but we absolutely cannot fill the emptiness of the person. If someone were to ask me suddenly: What is redemption? What purpose does it serve when humankind has arrived at a point where we either can do anything or it is only a matter of time before we are able to, I would answer: "Redemption? It is the remedy for loneliness," the one sickness in the face of which we have been and always will be impotent.

We are mistaken if we think that the other with whom we live in the closest possible contact can free us from our loneliness, that is, our fixation upon ourselves. The anxious and frantic gift of our total self to the other can generate the illusion that we have discovered and now see the other. But the other is nothing more than a plank that we hold on to for dear life. The strong and enfolding embrace with which we cling to the other can give the impression that we are total "otherness," but in time it becomes clear that the embrace is the deadly hold of a drowning person in which both he and his rescuer sink below the waves. Only the absolutely other can save us. Saint Teresa used to say that hell is the place where no one can love. And that is exactly what the inability to love is—the inability to see the other, to relate with the other as the "other distinct from me." I would dare say that if as adults we suffer from pathological loneliness, this means we have not been liberated from our own selves. Not to have found the other and the others in order to live the dimension of love (the escape from loneliness) does not depend on circumstances, lost opportunities, death, but simply on not having become liberated, on not having achieved maturity. All the rest that makes up the course of one's personal history can be more or less sad.

Events turn tragic; the encounter with the other or the others is joyful or sad, but it does not touch the most hidden depth, the center of loneliness or of communion where the self either remains helplessly alone or in intimate communion with the others.

The history of our relationship with others and with things can have a profound influence in our life. A lot depends on whether we have a joyful or melancholy temperament, but this cannot reach to the substance, the ontological base, of our self, the command post of our history, that is to say, whether we are to be slaves or free, sinners or redeemed, held fast in the contemplation of our navel or, on the other hand, to distinguish the other and be projected, "lost," in the history of others. The fact that we might call out to the other seductively or tearfully, that we would be willing to spend the night under her balcony in the hope that she would open the window, does not mean that we are capable of communion. We all have a need for security. And the more we feel strange and out of place, glimpsing that we are not where we should be or doing what we should, the more we look for security. A tree growing up off-center has to be propped up. To those who have not matured properly, who have not been liberated, others are not their communion but their props.

How tragic, neat, and simple is the law of our life; we use people and things either for communion or for security, and we relate to people either through communion or a need to be secure. There is no alternative. To feel secure, physical presence and bodily contact are indispensable because security is only on a shallow level. Communion goes much deeper.

Certainly, not being present physically takes away a dimension important to communion; it tends to make it rather sad and obscure. But it does not destroy it, it never leaves the person bereft of everything. Therefore others are necessary, but only the Redeemer is indispensable. We can turn around the phrase, famous at the moment because perhaps it strikes the fancy of the present very lonely generation, to read, "Other people are our hell." The others are our hell precisely because they are not "the others." My self is in hell because the *others are not different from me.* I see, I touch, I talk with many people, but not one of them is truly "other for me." They are a group of players that entitle me to use the word "action" for my little game, "existence" for my archaic self old before its time, "love" for my desire to cling to others for security. All the summonses that come from on high, from the United Nations or from the Vatican, all the protests, have to do necessarily with objects of the will; they outline options for peace and justice. But to change my own will, to give it a fundamentally different direction, means nothing more than to change myself, and this in the strict sense is impossible for us because we cannot get clear of the swamp by pulling on our bootstraps. We cannot will to change our will.

The external and historic control that keeps us in our infantile condition and unable to discover the other as "other" is to be found in political structures made in our image and likeness, narcissistic structures that rule out otherness. Every attempt at dialogue fails because there is an ontological incapacity for dialogue. We are reminded of a group of blind people taken out "to see the scenery." The discourse is pathetic because it gives expression to a necessary and unrealizable law. These seeming adults, who are really children, have great power in their hands, and everything they plan and produce bears within it the sign of non-otherness, of fixation in the self.

On the level of interpersonal love we have a coupling instead of a couple. On the political level, a dictatorship; leaders are not chosen for their support of a political program of liberation but for their personal power. Also involved are economic power, sensitivity to money, the possibility of being bought, the chance of becoming a world leader—and therefore, it should be said, the capacity for being a symbol that surpasses the substance.

If we could see what we are really doing and not what we think we are doing, we would discover that things have not changed since the time the pagan Roman hordes chased after sexual symbols, held aloft in homage; we now chase after the political leader. In the business world the same thing happens. We call it "private" enterprise, and there is something comical about that adjective. There are many who put their shoulder to the wheel of its progress. The noun "enterprise" to our mind means a collective effort, something that you cannot do alone. And the solitary, egocentric mogul who controls the business tells us, "Remember that you work for me—private enterprise." Production and profit do not go from the center out to the periphery, from the one to the many, but from the many to the one.

In international politics narcissism is called colonialism. In the colonialist relationship between the richer and more developed country—the country more adept at politics and diplomacy—and the poorer and younger nations—nations less capable of autonomy—the latter unfortunately become satellite states. They are not *identified as* "other countries"; they are run by the "narcissistic" state, caught up in grandiose contemplation of its own excrement. Its benefices, its warlike activities, its proposals for alliance, and its aggressions are all nothing more than different displays of the same pathological condition. As long as the satellite countries are not aware of this and continue to oscillate between enthusiastic hysteria brought on by the decision of the colonial masters to make heavy investments and chronic depression because the flood of gold is drying up, there is no hope for freedom.

In the field of religion, narcissism is expressed in adoration of structures. The "others," when they begin to agitate, are ground up by the structure—or else they are directly eliminated, because sometimes the structural machine does not have teeth strong enough to grind up hard bones.

If this is the human situation, there is no remedy. And all the congresses, the exhortations, the studies are worth nothing because they are put on the superficial level where we can accept or reject, say yes or no, but not on the real level where authentic and lasting decisions are made. It is impossible for us to free ourselves from our profound loneliness. By our own efforts we cannot reach the other. I am much impressed with the words of Saint Luke, which are not mythical but on the contrary have an incredible timeliness. The "poor" man says to the "rich" man, "Between you and us there is fixed a great abyss, so that those who might wish to cross from here to you cannot do so, nor can anyone cross from your side to us" (Lk 16,26). All the earth and all creation is in our hands, but *the possibility of loving is not in us.*

I believe that human love—that powerful awakener of the person—is a call, a moment of grace. It is Christ passing by, as Saint Augustine would say; it is the one occasion wherein we discover our impoverishment and our limitations, and in that moment is born the kind of humility that is the mark of faith, of the cry of faith: "I would like to love, but I don't know how." Experience teaches that there can be encounters of love that create very intense vibrations, and yet we do not discover the true "other" through them. The other becomes only a projection of the self, a way of going on with the game of loneliness.

I adopt the words of the Protestant theologian Ebling in *L'essence de la foi chrétienne:*

Therefore we give witness that faith is not something that is added to being a person. It is not a kind of luxury that only people who are gifted or demanding in the matter of religion can and should bestow upon themselves. Faith does nothing more than return us to our true humanity and let us become creatures and children of God in the unity that always occurs between creation and redemption. And this is because, in the area of faith, we are talking about people being human. Believers are not superhuman; rather, because they have arrived at truth, they are truly human. Faith is a determinant of what concerns us and even of what concerns us in an absolute way, that is, our salvation.

It is necessary that this message should reach all and that faith should cease to be looked upon as a "religious task," so that it will be seen as the condition for living and for being. Therefore redemption is not a sideline, a sort of additional project, but the essential and indispensable condition for us to become what we should be, that is, beings who come out of ourselves and project ourselves into the other who is distinct from ourselves.

So that the message will be accepted, it is necessary that

those who are in some way responsible give evidence with their lives of the value of being liberated, that is to say, that they be persons who have been liberated from their loneliness. The others—the community—are channels of grace, the direct road along which liberation, which only God can give, will come to me. And they are at the same time the sign, the proof that liberation has arrived. If I truly love, I discover the others in loving; and, in a certain sense, I believe in them. I make them others distinct from me; that is to say, I make evident the liberation they have received, their identity. The encounter with the others, my relationship with them, is the manifestation, the making visible and present, of the interior gift that I have received. Only in relationship is it revealed, does it come to light, that one has been "touched by God," liberated by this contact. Therefore the true discovery of the "other" is, at the same time, the discovery of God.

Our role is difficult and full of risks. Either we die, pitifully putrefied, without knowing love but only pluralistic falsifications that will never have the taste of the communion for which all of us were born. Or we lose our life in the moment in which the others—or the other, he who is "outside of me"—become a call. In this call we find the Savior, the offer of salvation. Whoever wishes to save his life must lose it. This is the basic statute of Christianity and a life-giving sociological law. But in order to lose one's own life—which is an adult, conscious act, inspired only by the need of the other—it is necessary to have gone beyond the infantile stage and to have ceased being anchored to one's own sex.

The literature about the human psyche holds in store for us the surprise of discovering that the fulminations of prophetic anger and the expressions of disdain that have appeared at certain times and in certain people as a rejection of an agreeable reality hide an unimaginable scientific rigor: "Those accustomed to dainty food perish in the streets; those brought up in purple now cling to ash heaps" (Lam 4,5). This is not vengeance; this is a *revelation*.

The man described in Luke's gospel is apparently enterprising and full of plans. We can imagine him surrounded by a panel of collaborators, the designer of the grain bins, the crew of builders to tear down and rebuild. As a matter of fact, I once saw this in the Austrian production of *Everyman*, staged with great visual beauty and very human touches—a kind of Greek tragedy. Nevertheless in real life the man of Luke's gospel is alone; apparently he makes plans for the future, but in reality he is playing a sordid and macabre game. For this reason much is made in the gospel of the "truth," of being "true to oneself"; Jesus is identified with the truth: the way, the life, and the truth. Because only the way in the truth is the real way, the way that goes forward and not round about in circles. And to come alive in the truth is the only way to live.

When we discover the real and are aware that all along we have been deceived, believing that we were telling the truth and "doing" the truth when in fact we were falsifying it, we blame creation for the deceit. This error of perspective explains in part a "spiritual" literature of maledictions and condemnations of material things; this is antibiblical. In the Bible the Creator is represented as standing back for a moment from creation, like an artist, to admire and enjoy it. The gospel stresses this optimism and the joy of contemplating things which, in spite of their ephemeral existence, reveal eternal beauty to us.

Nevertheless, through an error similar to the pre-Copernican error—and perhaps harder to take in its consequences—we unload on the other, the one who is outside of our self, the responsibility for failing to see, for deceiving us, for doing one thing while believing we are doing another. Woman as a symbol of creation, as the synthesis of the dialectical other, has often been the victim of this kind of condemnation. "You have no right to talk, you who have seduced and deceived me." To a greater or lesser degree this judgment is at the heart of the man-woman relationship, whether in the case of the Fathers of the church or of the Makarite Indians who leave the women outside the door of the roundhouse where the community meets. And aggressiveness, which goes hand in hand with eroticism, is aggravated owing to these feelings of blame and retaliation. The results of this serious error of perspective are evident and we all carry them within ourselves.

That the things that come from the hand of the Creator are good in themselves is a fact we are now rediscovering in our time. Perhaps we never accepted this before with such conviction because we lacked the right perspective, like the pre-Copernicans who discovered correct hypotheses but lacked scientific arguments to defend them. Even the spiritual person has arrived at the point of being able to see the beauty of the world, but there are very few who have glimpsed it outside a setting of aggressiveness and fear. For centuries our culture was oppressed by the notion of nature as deceiver. It might be said that it was in vain that Saint Paul heard in the inner depths of creation the groaning of a nature violated and alienated by human beings, who do not "see" or "understand." I have set myself the task of rereading certain ascetical pages with a changed perspective; some are still valid, others no longer are.

The worst thing is that the discovery of that "deceit," the "trap" set by creatures, leads us to conclusions that create in us a proud and irresponsible attitude. All our proposals for conversion can go on being false because they are directed to what does not need conversion, that which should not change.

Freud says that in a relatively short time human pride has suffered three major setbacks. The first was the discovery of Copernicus that the earth is not the center of the cosmos; the second, Darwin's discovery that the gulf between human beings and other creatures is only apparent, however well publicized by human pride; the third, Freud's own discovery that consciousness is only the tip of an immense iceberg. We should say of the third that it is not a disillusionment but rather a discovery that holds the same value as the theory of heliocentrism. Only it is necessary for us to rethink within this perspective all our decisions, the whole of our ethical and spiritual life. I understand the danger of "subjectivism" in this, but to ignore this Freudian perspective would be parallel to an effort to construct a physics, a cosmology and, therefore, an anthropology on the hypothesis that the earth is the center of the universe.

We can no longer talk about the "spiritual life" in the sense in which the phrase has been used until now, because it seems evident that the human self germinates in darkness in a very rich but treacherous humus that conditions it. The enemy is not outside me but within me. Am I capable of a creative encounter? Can I draw near to a person and produce in that person a spurt of growth in being; or am I, on the contrary, only capable of brutalizing, mutilating, and destroying? Am I able to see the flowers of the field that are as marvelous as the cloak of Solomon; or, on the contrary, can I see the meadows only as economic entities, commercial objects?

Things are not *dung*. The face radiant with the smile of youth is not a *display of worms* even though pre-Copernican saints may have said so and even though beauty is subject to the ravages of time. The grass that Christ contemplated was green but would also wither away. Nevertheless he contemplated it full of joy and sealed it in the eternal moment of its beauty, deeming it more beautiful than the cloak of Solomon. It is I myself, my eyes, my "regression"—my fixation in a stage that I have biologically long since gone beyond—that prevents me from seeing things "as they are," in their reality. Because I do not see things "as they are" but only in their appearance, my relating to them is false, "alienated." I do not attain to making "use of the world as though I were not using it" (1 Cor 7,31). Only the salvation proclaimed by the gospel can liberate me from this "alienation." Marx throws me at the feet of Christ. I have to be re-created, to be liberated from my old self.

The invitations to free ourselves from our old self take on a new meaning: "You must lay aside your former way of life and the old self which deteriorates through illusion and desire, and acquire a fresh, spiritual way of thinking. You must put on that new man created in God's image, whose justice and holiness are born of truth" (Eph 4,22–24). I repeat—so that I will not be misunderstood—that this kind of renewal cannot be found apart from concrete relationships. But the center is always the person. The result of conversion is not an idol-smashing pessimism or a witch-burning zeal; it is a smiling and hopeful lovingness, a new capacity for accepting the other and the others: "What God has purified you are not to call unclean" (Acts 11,9).

If the only thing that happens to a convert is to feel hatred for the world and those in it, then the conversion is really doubtful. In fact conversion transforms completely the level and the methods of essential human relationships. Some cases are understandable because relationships exist that are unreformable and because the self that is born cannot enter into the free and mature stage of its life without uncertainties, residues of fear, and guilt complexes. I shall always remember a picture of conversion that is especially graphic. After having moistened with saliva the eyes of the blind man of Bethsaida, Jesus asks him whether he can see anything, and the man answers: "I can see people, but they look like walking trees!" (Mk 8,22–25). After the second imposition of hands the man sees perfectly. Conversion is the beginning of the road to freedom and to loving kindness toward others and toward the world. Health recovered is precisely the ability to see beings as they are; it is the end to alienation.

I insert here a reflection on a concept that has entered into ordinary speech. Is it we who alienate the world and the political structure or is it the other way round? Certainly there is an interplay, but the seat and center of alienation is the person. Alienation is sin—that is, the refusal to see the other and the others—and for this reason things are seen and used apart from their own meaning. When we hear it said that capitalism and consumer society alienate the person, we must not forget that they are a projection of alienated people. That very phrase—consumer society—is striking; it is self-denunciatory. This is the phrase we use to designate a narcissistic culture that turns in upon itself, instead of using a phrase indicative of creation, of intelligent planning for the future.

Alienated persons can project themselves only into alienated structures. Ignorance of the other as other, as the "thou" of dialogue—the bearer of liberation if I recognize this other as distinct from me—is projected into a structure that suppresses the other as a dialectical terminus, as a call to get outside myself, to deny myself, to die in order to be reborn and, therefore, as a bearer of real grace. Things do not change, however much the other is suppressed by weaponry, by political power, or by doctrinaire terrorism.

It is naive today to speak of a free society. *Free societies do not exist* because, in our culture, there are no free people—except, perhaps, one here, one there. It is true that to break down individualistic structures, to tumble the infantile castle in which we are prisoners and put us out among the others, obliging us to see them, can be an entering wedge. Snatching away from the children the stock certificates with which they play their macabre game may drive them into the desert of desperation, but it can also put them on the road to humility. It can help them to see that they have been playing with excrement. To force alienated people to become aware that others exist and that the others are at the door, threatening them, can provoke an aggressive and violent response; but it can also make them discover that they are not alone and that loneliness is not the inescapable human condition but a pathological state.

It is true that political or social revolutions in themselves cannot resolve the problem of alienation, cannot prevent people from being seen as trees, perhaps as trees that can be cut down and sold. A person who, looking out the window, sees the others at the door can either run out to welcome them or shoot at them. This fact need not discourage political and revolutionary initiative that hopes to bring about justice by liquidating structures that are alienating. But the initiative of faith and redemption should not be absent. The Christian initiative is not just a plan to make things pleasant, but the proclamation and the fact of salvation carried to the very center of alienation. The political initiative ought to become, at the same time, a bearer of faith and a beginning of redemption.

In passing we have seen that to have a sense of history, of the present, is a sign that I have a genuine relationship with the other. For the others to "be," it is necessary that they be alive and not dead. If they are dead, they are a dead projection of a dead self, that is, frozen in a stage where time has passed them by. The other, to be other, has to be a vital, creative, provocative relationship. My dialectical terminus is opposite, is a negation of my self. To put ourselves on philosophical ground, we can take another look at a meditation of Saint Thomas on the Trinity. The Persons are equal and distinct, united by the love that keeps them in opposition. Their being is love and opposition because opposition is the only condition making them distinct and love is the only condition making them equal. And what is this humus in which the person lives, grows, and remains the "other" if it is not history? Therefore the Christian who sees the other as an object of compassion, of do-goodism, as a "poor little thing" that should be helped does not really see the other. The neighbor in this case is the pretext for giving food and space to the self locked up in itself, whether it is called the ego, the id, or the super-ego. Many altruistic discussions, if they are analyzed, reveal a kind of non-altruism, the total absence of the other. Those who have clearly decided what they should give to their neighbors and make them take it whether they like it or not because they know what is good for their neighbors—these "benefactors" are as much alone as the man in Luke. They are just as egotistical, even though it would seem otherwise.

Whoever has discovered the other accepts the challenge of history; that is, such a one is ready for the creation that is born as the fruit of the encounter with the other. The sign of having come out of myself is precisely the acceptance of the challenge of time; liberation is the rejection of non-time, of the old state in which my self was frozen. For this reason I maintain, with an ever-growing conviction, that "saints," those liberated by the Lord, are the historic people who live in their time and accept the other as a challenge, as a companion in the search. The Epistle to the Hebrews states emphatically, and perhaps with a meaning we still have not grasped to the fullest: "When he says, 'a new covenant,' he declares the first one obsolete. And what has become obsolete and has grown old is close to disappearing" (Heb 8,13). No one can escape from this human risk; everyone must be freed from the prison of the self. And not one, nor a hundred thousand, have this possibility of freeing us from the hell of our loneliness.

Let us go back to the man in Luke. He interests us because we are always running into him, and maybe something of him is in us all. Jesus confronts him and judges him. "You fool! This very night your life shall be required of you." Every word is in its place and hits the nail on the head. Our man seems to be astute, prudent, and far-seeing, but in fact he is stupid. He seems to be an important person, but in reality he is a child. There are wise and outstanding people who do not understand the meaning of life, and there are poor and humble people who do indeed understand it. The poor cannot escape the desperate needs of those who live near by. There is nothing they can put between themselves and the others. They lack symbols with which to cover up their infantile behavior. They cannot simulate wisdom and love because they do not have the symbols for it, not having learned them either in school or in church. They have to stand before the others defenseless and whole. The poor, too, are in need of redemption. The so-called "good people" who are liberated are nonexistent. But lowliness—poverty as it is understood in the gospel—is this not already a sign of liberation?

The drama of the man in Luke could not have a worse epilogue. It is necessary to remove it from its moralistic and superficial schematization. The parable has been employed to talk about hell and to frighten Christians into taking care of their souls, whereas the epilogue to the story is much deeper and more complex. The man has made a plaything out of time; his game is possible if time can be made an abstraction. He has not realized that he is "archaic," that he is frozen in an age that no longer exists. His discourse, which seems very concrete because he has taken note of the location of his grain bins and of the hugeness of his harvest, is really abstract. His goods are not the lifeblood of a community on the march. They do not become food for humanity. They stagnate and become a morass where the lonely man says to himself, "You have blessings in reserve for years to come. Relax, eat heartily, drink well, enjoy yourself." But time has betrayed him. He does not observe this because he has stood apart from the others to protect his self; the awesome enemy is not part of his plans.

When locking the door, he has given no thought to the fact that the enemy lies in wait outside and may break in at any moment. Fixed in an age that has become increasingly more remote—like rubble, like a ruin—he has been unable to preserve the sense of time.

Time is visible in plants, in flowers, in the human physiological seasons, in history, in the process of liberation. But it does not enter into the deep recesses of the infantile self, which grows old without undergoing any real change. "This night, now." Time comes foward to meet him, not as a bearer of life but as a messenger of death. He does not know the kind of time that brings the newness of spiritual growth in its stages from unconsciousness to consciousness and on to a "greater consciousness." For him time is dead; it is a murky atmosphere that encloses him like a turtle in its shell.

"This very night your life shall be required of you." Who? Who is it that is going to "require" of him? It is the "others," those he has not known how to identify, those whom he has not seen. While he was caught up in his narcissistic game, time and the others escaped him because the others are in time. They are the others inasmuch as they accept their risk, inasmuch as they live within their law of growth, not biological but human. They are the others on the march. When the self is outside the law of growth, they are instruments of security and support. Nevertheless the others exist, and even when they become instruments they have their space and their history. And they rise up against whoever has made them instruments. The others require your soul of you; the Greek text uses *psyken*, your psyche, your self. Treated as things, oppressed by your false and archaic self—frozen in the age of infancy, incapable of otherness—they will require your "I," the center of your person. They will require it not as a claim of love, of dialogue; they will require it to execute it, to destroy it.

The deep self, center of our person, is the center of relationship; according to the paradoxical meaning of the gospel it must be lost in order to be saved. Either there is a relationship of communion or there will be hatred and vengeance. We are at the root of the drama of the world, of wars, of violent oppression, of the consumer society. The violence of people upon things, upon the community, of man upon woman. If the other does not come to liberate me, our human condition is incurable. We are capable of eroticism but not love. To find communion we work tenaciously at communication. We have manipulated time and space so much that what were obstacles to communication have now become insignificant elements. We share as televiewers in the walk of the astronaut on the moon. We walk, we touch, we see what he sees, and this is marvelous. But it is not communion.

Everyone dreams about peace, in the East as well as in the West, because we are all agreed that the only pleasant way to live is to be where one loves and is loved. But, incapable of otherness, we confuse peace with identification. A world at peace would therefore be a world in which everyone thought as I did. The opposition of the self and the thou—the thou which is not the self and the self which is not the thou, which are in irreducible opposition—is the image of the world. It is the law with which and on which the world has been built.

The peace that this person who is an adult and a child at the same time dreams about has as a prior condition that the "thou" be equal to the "I," and only if the "thou" becomes "I" will the "thou" be allowed to exist. This is what happens on the level of the couple, in business and in politics, both internal and international. With the elimination of space and time, communication is now seen as an instrument to do away with the "thous." A small sign of this: Any telegram going from Buenos Aires to Paris or Rome has to go through New York. Is this a technical problem? Yes, a technical problem that reflects the psychological state of the person.

Communication, for the moment, is not communion; on the contrary it does nothing more than increase the anger of the poor. They are aware that the elimination of time and space brings the slaves ever closer to the masters and gives them the opportunity of ruling the slaves more quickly and more easily anywhere in the world. Nevertheless the world is ready to take up arms against the method of "identification," which is now referred to hypocritically by the labels "peace," "obedience," "integration," "economic aid." Perhaps the destiny of each generation is not only the one intuited by Teilhard de Chardin—to grow toward an "increase in awareness"—but also to delve deep in the search for the roots of evil.

The French Revolution revealed the macroscopic injustice of society wickedly divided into three separate groups. The socialist revolution goes a step further in its analysis of the causes: The evil that lies at the root of society is the unjust distribution of wealth. The personalist and communitarian revolution—our revolution—will discover even deeper down the inability of people, of the political sphere, of government, to relate to the thou.

It can be said that history faces in different stages the great human problem of being—relating to things—and of relating to our equals. The historic theme of tomorrow, which we will leave open to our children, will be loneliness and therefore relationship. The problem of God, freed from all the cosmic implications, of all causality, will appear with utter simplicity as the indispensable absolute, here, at this point. Therefore I believe that in our time a great Christian age will begin. Not in the sense that Christians will be able to solve political and philosophical problems but in the sense that we will be borne along to the discovery of the ultimate stronghold where the absolutely Other will be revealed to us.

4

Our Judges

There was a man there named Zacchaeus, the chief tax collector and a wealthy man. He was trying to see what Jesus was like, but being small of stature, was unable to do so because of the crowd. He ran on in front, then climbed a sycamore tree which was along Jesus' route, in order to see him. When Jesus came to the spot he looked up and said, "Zacchaeus, hurry down. I mean to stay at your house today."

He quickly descended and welcomed him with delight. When this was observed, everyone began to murmur, "He has gone to a sinner's house as a guest."

Zacchaeus stood his ground and said to the Lord: "I give half my belongings, Lord, to the poor. If I have defrauded anyone in the least, I pay him back fourfold."

Jesus said to him: "Today salvation has come to this house, for this is what it means to be a son of Abraham. The Son of Man has come to search out and save what is lost" (Lk 19,2–10).

As we saw, the kind of personage depicted in the twelfth chapter of Luke is lost at sea; things ruin him—or better still, fail to liberate him. Locked irrevocably in his infantile stage, he cannot be reached by the other and the others. Those who have the message and the grace of salvation come at the last moment only to announce the disaster. "This very night your life shall be required of you." Nothing and nobody has gotten into this pitiful life, so sure of itself, to break its rhythm, to destroy this peace that is only a provisional kind of security gained by money and withdrawn from time and space.

Further on in the pages of Luke we encounter a quite similar person. He is also a rich man, one of the leading publicans. The protective wall around his self is brought down all of a sudden: the Other invades his life like a hurricane. He is the only person in the four gospels who freely takes the initiative of meeting the Master. He has nothing to say and nothing to ask. Nicodemus, on the other hand, has a doctrinal curiosity. He probably comes in the role of an inquisitor, and he is not unarmed. He has heard people talking here and there about Jesus of Nazareth and he wants to get a good look at what he is all about. He does not seem driven by metaphysical anguish. Because it takes the form of dialogue, the encounter is an exchange of opinions under the pretext of seeking information. If this is the same Nicodemus we meet in the account of Christ's death, surely the first encounter was not simply a press conference.

But Zacchaeus, less learned, less interested in metaphysical problems, has a strange desire. According to the text of Luke, he wanted to "see him." All of a sudden he has an appetite for the Other. Granted, even this desire, this curiosity, could have been a caprice of the self. The self needs the other because the self runs the whole gamut of emotions: love, hatred, remorse, lust, cruelty, crying over cruelty. This whole comedy involving one actor needs back-up people when the actor is not the only one obliged to develop the affective growth of the self. The other could become for Zacchaeus a "distraction"; his curiosity could be that of Herod who brought Jesus before him to see Jesus perform. But Zacchaeus is forced to get outside himself. He cannot "bring the other before him"; he is obliged to go to him.

This is probably the psychological translation of the Exodus, model of all relationships with the Other. Only God can be the irreducible Other for us. Woman, nature, things stir up and challenge the person as the other distinct from the self. And this is the easy obvious way that the poor and lowly have for escaping from the death-dealing love of self, almost without being aware of it. Hiding behind this challenge is the irreducible Other, the one who has the exclusive and definitive power to liberate us from the self.

We have been experiencing these days, at the level of the poor, the small but great event of encounter. In our "desert" of Suriyaco, in a house like all the rest, surrounded by fertile land abandoned for many decades (because of an inhuman urbanization, not planned but inspired by a get-rich-quick scheme), we have had various visitors. The "Herods" looking for a change from their deadly boredom; the "Nicodemuses" interested in metaphysics; the prisoners of the concentration camp of their "self" who need to unload on others the results of the rejection of their devouring monomania. In conversation, they all come up immediately with their personal history. Those who know the secrets of science and of the economy try to help our impoverished imagination with obscure and very complicated plans which will all work out so simply because they are friends of a general, or because they have a cousin who holds an important post in the Inter-American bank and, well, last Monday they had lunch at the Plaza Hotel with the President of the Republic.

One day there appeared on the horizon a poor man who had come a distance of ten miles with a yoke of oxen and a rustic wooden plow. He asked us where he was supposed to plow and quietly went to work. He stayed until sundown, leaving the small field neatly plowed and ready for the seed. To our insistent offers to pay him for his work he responded with the nobility that the great of this world reveal only in moments of immense danger: He did not want any money; he didn't want anything, only our friendship. I learned a lot from this "other": What the real meaning of aid to underdeveloped countries is, our "charity"; what we have hidden under the words "apostolate," "conversion," "evangelization"; what we have brought and given and tried to impose with a smile or with force, with arms or with words. We have not brought the Other because the concrete other did not interest us—the other we should have reached out to, touched, raised up in his concrete history, which is the history of his real need. We were not interested because the other is the negation of our self. He is not someone asking us for something.

Even to this genuine brother who, with his oxen, brought us an evangelization, the service he performed represented in its social context something that went far beyond his work, the time lost with us, the "charity" done us. It meant the destruction of the myth about the simple and innocent "cunning" of the poor. It constituted a break with his own primitive economic structure and with the laws of every country. Work and time are paid for with money—a lot or a little, depending on the astuteness, the power, the greater or lesser sensitivity of the individual. But no, this man came looking for the "thou," the "other," and he was able to find him precisely at the point where the latter was as defenseless and as poor as himself. He was the "other," the one for whom we are here and whom we one day hope to reach because of our "training." He came to us asking nothing, without any recommendation, only for friendship. His work was stripped of any economic meaning in order to be translated into the language of friendship.

In writing this I feel I am intellectualizing. I feel that anyone who is not looking desperately for Christ in the poor will not be able to understand it. But I want to do it because I am dazzled by an intuition—the hint of an answer to a question that has always worried me: "And who is your neighbor?" Who is the other?

Zacchaeus gives the impression that he is looking for the other; indeed the search begins at the moment when a desire for another dimension than the economic creeps into the life of a contented rich man. Presently the yearning for the other becomes stronger than all the rest of his desires; it is a force that obliges him to get out of his self. And, perhaps for the first time, he bumps into the wall of helplessness. He was unable to see Jesus because he was small of stature and because the Prophet was surrounded by a crowd. Possibly it was not only the obstacle presented by the large crowd which prevented him from approaching Jesus; it may also have been the fact that he was a man the crowd had no use for. Helplessness now obliged him to clarify the motive behind his strange desire, so alien to his usual whims. In the first instance, what had arisen in Zacchaeus was the plain and simple decision to go to meet the Other. In reading the gospel there is no need to be sidetracked, for very often the details are the marrow of the story. The text says that he just wanted to see Jesus. He had no clear, fixed idea of the Other.

Herod summons Jesus because he is interested in magic; to keep alive, his self has dug a tunnel of mystery where he takes refuge to hide himself from the irreducible Other. God is admitted into this hiding place only on the condition that he play the part of magician. The other is not Other when he is someone we expect to meet, when we know ahead of time what he will ask of us, when we can foresee exactly what he wants of us and we go forth to the encounter, already bringing what he will ask of us. The *Other is the negation of our self* and, therefore, he is the only force that can move us and give us genuine time and space and history. In order to be Other, he should not be capable of being assimilated by our "self"; from the moment when he becomes assimilable—when he no longer challenges me, when he ceases to be a "mystery," to be a "judge"—he ceases to be Other. If I can enmesh him, lock him up in my "self," if I already know what he is asking of me, he is no longer the Other. God is not Other for the Pharisee in the parable (Lk 18,10) because the Pharisee imagines that he is accepted by a god who is pleased with his alms, his prayers, his posture of piety. In reality he is embracing a god made to *his own* likeness, within the walls of his own self. In order not to tear down the walls of his own self, in order not to enter into the arena of history, he needs to annul the Other; and to annul the Other, religiosity is a more radical course than atheism. Religiosity annuls the one great negation and all the lesser negations. It closes the door through which the Other might be able to enter by surprise. The atheist closes the door but does not block up the holes. The publican does not know everything; he does not play the game of reducing the Other to impotence from the moment the latter introduces negation into his life. The Pharisee forestalls negation, his life is without it. His life can be lonely, boring, desperate, but it can have no substance nor be qualitatively other because the Other is excluded. The publican adopts a stance of surrender; he is ready to renounce the direction of his life. Whoever has gone deeply into a relationship knows that the renunciation of initiative is the greatest act of courage because it means going out to meet death with open eyes. It is madness, because it is a negation of all the laws inscribed in the structure of the person. Zacchaeus does not know what he wants of the Other nor what the Other requires of him.

The danger in all religions is to know what the Other wants of me, to think that I have what the Other is demanding, to estimate my wealth, my power over the Other. To eliminate this danger I must go through a stage of total doubt that leads to my touching the existence of the Other. This was the torment of Saint Theresa of Lisieux—the presence of the Other that exists beyond the "dark clouds," beyond the total doubt that envelops her and that is illuminated by a tenuous light, barely visible, barely sufficient so as not to interrupt the search. Her relationship with the Other is no longer entrusted to things, to the means of relating. The Other has become so distant, so unattainable, that all the means are lost sight of as well as all roads to reunion with the Other. She waits like someone caught in a storm and biding time until the sun reappears. All has disappeared except this tenuous certainty that the Other will make himself visible when and how he decides to. She has lost the measure of time and space and therefore cannot attain the Other.

Zacchaeus is already poor by the time he climbs the tree. He is totally ignorant of the way to draw near to the Other; having no experience, he is guided only by an indefinite desire because in reality he does not know who the Other is. He is naked; he does not even have the asset of the poor—the need that calls for dialogue. My very need can be a force, a last refuge of the self which knows what it needs, which wants what it is lacking and gives to the other the power it does not have within the self. Zacchaeus goes forth to the encounter, to which he is mysteriously called from the depth of his being, in absolute poverty.

The Other enters my life to call me to an unknown destiny, to an unconditional surrender, to a renunciation of all primary and daily needs, even the purest and deepest behind which the self can hide itself in a kind of ultimate bastion. For this reason "many are called but few are chosen"; the majority turn back. When the Other destroys one by one all the roads that branch out from the self because they lead nowhere, most people turn back. The emptiness that lies between the end of my road and the arrival point of the Other is death, and few have the courage to surrender themselves spontaneously to death. This is the usual reason why religion is the refuge of the weak rather than the strong, of the superficial rather than those who wish to be real. In the face of death everything is cheap. He who is Love emerges only with the death of self, and this kind of death frightens us. Only grace—the salvation that comes to us from the Other—can give us courage.

Zacchaeus is unaware of what is needed for encountering Christ, and therefore his initiative—so childish, so funny, so meager—is really immense. He is drawn to the Other as to a splendid and terrifying abyss. In order to know who He is, he has to get away from the crowd, climb up into the branches, and wait. The Other might go in another direction, might not notice him, not see him. Attentive to whoever is dragging Him here and there, ready to listen to someone with a sick child or to someone who needs his sight restored, Jesus might not attach any importance to this unknown hidden amidst the foliage of a tree and impelled merely by a desire to see him pass by.

We can only wait for the Other and look for him from afar. The love that is real is made of poverty and impotence. Until it is poverty and impotence it is not "otherness"; it is nothing more than a projection of the self. The Other will never walk the roads I chart for him—"my roads are not your roads." The only attitude that will attract him is my readiness and my waiting. The gospel frequently talks about the attitude of the person who waits. The good and faithful servant is the one who patiently and truly waits. Whoever tires of waiting and fills the dreary emptiness with speculations about the hidden intentions of the master who may arrive at any moment, instead of being patient is a servant who is not in readiness.

The Other walks along the tree-lined road, sees Zacchaeus in his observation post, and invites him to come down. "Hurry down, I mean to stay at your house today." It is not a passing visit, the visit of a miracle-worker who lays on hands. He is the friend who is going to stay at his house. He does not go to leave anything; he goes to be the Other to Zacchaeus, the one who will bring him out of his self, the liberator. And Zacchaeus comes down, runs in front of Jesus, happy, liberated, ready to extend a cordial welcome.

We can fantasize a bit here about this account and suppose that the decision to go forth to the encounter with the Other was not an occurrence without preliminaries. We can imagine long and baffling suffering, disillusionment over the limitations and value of everything, the long, drawn-out pain of living. At a given moment, this pain, which veils every human experience in sadness, homes in on an intuition. Maybe there is someone who can liberate him from his profound loneliness, someone who can help him discover what love really is and knock down the wall he collides with every time he tries to love, someone who would come to him and love him as he is, Zacchaeus, apart from his wealth and the stigma of being a usurer, a thou who would discover and descend to the depth, to that unsettling depth he had never been able to reach either in times of sorrow or of happiness, to this depth to which the self cannot descend because it is that which is before, outside of its time, in the "beginning." The future fills us with fear, perhaps because it is a projection of the past, of that which is before our history and which will always remain apart from it. As long as we are not freed from this fear, the self will try to flee desperately into a false history that is not its own. I must discover the thou who has always wanted me, who has left no empty space, who knows me "since before I existed in my mother's womb."

Today Zacchaeus feels that this emptiness has been filled. Not only his material house is inhabited but also his interior house, the house where his self had lived with a stranger, where, unknown and estranged, he had never found security. This explains his lack of the profound joy to which we have a right even within our history—the joy of discovering that our existence is rooted in love. When we find ourself rooted in this eternal and tenacious love and live this revelation, everything becomes relative. Nothing, no fragment, is to be despised, because everything is a detail of this initial love. Nevertheless everything becomes relative because we discover that the only root of happiness is to find ourselves loved before our time. The color and taste of the joys of life begin with the joy of being. Every kind of happiness rests on insecurity, on emptiness, until we discover the thou that precedes our existence. When we discover it, we understand why the Other is called the Beginning and the End, the Alpha and the Omega. This is not a theological or metaphysical nicety; it is the only condition on which the Other can be truly the Other and can endow the self with that mysterious security that makes it able to attempt the great adventure, the real and most important exodus.

After Zacchaeus's encounter that day with the Other, everything unfolds very logically. Luke records the episode that moves this history of liberation forward. The crowd that is following the guest of Zacchaeus gathers around the house. And they begin to protest and to criticize because "he has gone to a sinner's house as a guest." It is as though, after the Other, the others came into the solitary life of Zacchaeus. The Other enters as a friend—"I mean to stay at your house today" —without laying down conditions, without pouncing on him because of his sinful condition. Finally, he calls him by his name, Zacchaeus. The others come into his life violently and unfairly. For them he is not Zacchaeus, the name by which the Other has called him; he is a sinful man, a rich man guilty of exploitation, someone to be avoided at all costs.

It cannot be the first time that Zacchaeus was singled out for scorn. He always bears the sign of apartness because he is separated from the chosen people. I have lived through this religious situation in Algeria: Those who drink whiskey are guilty of legal impurity; they are not allowed in the mosque and their co-religionists point a finger at them. That one is a sinner; he has no right to pray. This is a distressing kind of ostracism because belonging to a religion is identified with belonging to a nation. Nevertheless, in Zacchaeus there has occurred a decisive and radical change of perspective. Before, he looked out upon the others from the observation post of his own self: aggressiveness or compassion, reprisal or pardon —they were all judged from the standpoint of self, as a means of defense. Zacchaeus had to keep in mind the others, who existed and who judged him, even before the great day of the encounter. They were obstacles who disturbed and endangered his immense loneliness. And because of this strange and inexplicable destiny he both hated his loneliness and defended it with all his energies. The others existed only as a menace: They might plot against him either through "kindness" or by force. Today, now that he has known the Other and has come out of himself to know and accept Him, he sees the others in their true perspective. Zacchaeus has become "other distinct from himself" and therefore is able to see his whole life from the other side, from the point of view of the others.

It seems clear to me what the reason is for the two decisions offered to the one who has found the Other. First of all there is the reality of evil, the immense and frightening emptiness of life. Others judge superficially, in negative terms, the experience of those who have found the Other; they see it as a form of "necrophilia," love of death, of nothingness, and worse. These phrases do not arise from the confrontation of one's own unrighteous life with the perfections of God. Anyway, who understands the perfection of God? To imagine it, one would have to stretch one's own "perfections" to the infinite; and the attempt would do no more than inflate one's own ego, something impossible for anyone who has really discovered the Other. This discovery represents a change of perspective: I see clearly that all my "perfections" and my righteousness are false because they are motivated by non-love: otherness, the instrument of love, is not functioning. Everything, the little lies of pride, the act of self-indulgence as well as the initiatives I considered "good"—they all seem to me emptiness, sin, because everything is inspired by non-love.

The total and global devaluation that comes about through the "change of perspective" is different from the paralyzing anguish that is born of guilt complexes. The anguish I am talking about is bathed in joy. We cannot make this discovery without a liberation; we cannot think and act differently if we are still in the perspective of the self. The person who is really spiritual, not through a refinement of the self but through a liberating invasion of the self by the Other, is a person at peace. Peace is here understood as that discerning joy which makes us see, with "natural" logic, the nothingness of the past that preceded our liberation, our discovery of the Other.

Christians are not "perfect" in the sense that they try by every possible means and by all kinds of daring acrobatics to disconnect the self from what is base and "earthly"; Christians are those who walk toward perfection because they move in a new perspective that is the perspective of love. They have not discovered perfection; they have discovered the Other, and their lives are entrusted forever to this great friendship. The concept of the "imitation of Christ" can help aggrandize and inflate the ego, and in fact that is what happens. I am not the one who should decide to imitate Christ as a Person who is outside of me and has performed in a certain way; this can produce a superego that is hypocritical and inexorably closed to the other. It should rather be the Other who brings me to his perspective. Saint Paul claims to be an imitator of Christ inasmuch as he discovers in his life marks, signs, that parallel the life of Christ. In reality Paul sees himself as a prisoner, enveloped in Christ.

Christ is the only irreducible Other for us. This is why he is our only savior. There are not two salvations because really there is no great variety of sins; there is nothing more than the history of liberation, discovery, and surrender of the self to the other.

The other aspect that becomes evident in the decision is the option in favor of the poor. This decision can also prove to be false and hypocritical. It is even more dangerous because it gives a greater margin of security to the self. All that is decided for the benefit of the self, from its perspective, is equally false whether it be prayer or the quest for a woman, charity or the exploitation of one person by another through labor and the economy. We can understand perfectly how capitalists would be prodigal with their money, since the crime and its expiation are the two movements of the self, locked up in its concentration camp. The one complements the other. They are like the two movements of the heart and the blood. Exploitation and charity are the two sides of the same coin. Changing from one class to another, passing from the rich class to the poor, can be a complementary movement, the law of self-preservation.

Those who lack otherness end up doing damage wherever they go and in whatever they do, just as when I've become disoriented and still try to move about in a dark room, I break things. And the voice of the one who lives with me pleads with me: "Stop, don't move! Wait till I put on the light." I would like to say to people all fired up about the Third World or the world of the poor: "Stop, don't move! You are not the ones who can welcome the poor. It is the poor who must welcome you." "I mean to stay at your house today." This situation would be tragic if redemption did not come out of it, if the Other had not come in search of the self, incurably enclosed in itself and incapable of otherness, of true otherness. People live out the same drama on the personal level and on the international political level. People project their small histories onto the structure that is created in their image.

This manner of giving is the diastole, the second moment, of taking, of stealing. I remember a violent discussion in Fribourg, Switzerland, between two Latin American youths and an outstanding theologian. The two Latin Americans had no rational arguments, they did not know by heart the Scholastic syllogisms to defend their thesis, which was a rejection of almsgiving as a virtue because the alms were gathered by theft in the first place. They were giving the theologian a good argument, because if theft is involved, restitution is called for. We are finite and therefore can be converted and healed. To attribute to ourselves a hellish unchangeableness is to be ignorant of our extreme psychic instability, our emotional and, therefore, rational instability. Nevertheless the intuition is fair: Even restitution is not free of guilt, because it is decided upon from the standpoint of the self. It is a movement from within a self that has not discovered otherness. And thus everything is infected.

The punishment of the "rich in spirit," according to the gospel, consists in a radical incapacity for friendship; therefore all the symbols of friendship—a letter, a gift, an act of charity—go out from the self to the others.

Those priests, monks, and nuns are right when they tell me that the rich are unhappier than the poor. And they tell me this defensively, to save their structures, firmly anchored in the little ports of the rich. The least evangelized are the rich, certainly, but to evangelize them directly, from within, to address myself to their self, is to *worsen the situation*. What we call evangelization only adds wood to the fire because it favors the second movement of the self, their need for expiation, the masochistic side of the self. Even certain structures of the church are projections of the capitalist self, caught up in contemplation of its excrement. The most visible expression of this—and perhaps the least hypocritical—is the great monasteries adjacent to palaces where the prince, tormented by guilt because he had poisoned his wives and political enemies, used to stroll in cloisters where penitential psalms were being recited. Things have not changed much; only appearances have become plebeian and have been laicized.

Jesus does not evangelize Zacchaeus. The real evangelization takes place in the words with which Jesus reveals the meaning of this happening. He allows others to enter into his life—the others, insolent and, at times, unrighteous. The salvation of Zacchaeus is to rediscover the others; they are the ones who must accept him, decide his destiny, look at him from their viewpoint and judge whether he has become "other" or if he is still locked up in his concentration camp. The others throw stones at the windows, make their judgment heard in the room of the Guest. "He is a sinner, a thief." But Zacchaeus now has a new perspective; he has seen his life for an instant through a new lens. "I will give half of my belongings, Lord, to the poor. If I have defrauded anyone in the least, I will pay him back fourfold." The silence of Christ is to be noted. He does not become an intermediary between Zacchaeus and the crowd. He does not say a word. Everything is decided between Zacchaeus and the others on the basis of the judgment made by the others.

In the house of a rich person I have at times lived through the episode of Zacchaeus. The maid who serves at the table approaches the master or the mistress and whispers, "There is someone at the door." "The usual beggars," says the mistress, with the self-satisfied air of one who feels herself to be indispensable. The master takes out his wallet and extracts some money, remarking that one would need all the funds of the Bank of America to take care of the needs that are becoming ever more pressing. The self goes serenely from the dining room to the door, personally or by the long hand of the servant (depending on the social class of the household). In fact, the whole transaction goes from the self to the self. The Other has not accepted the self, and the state of emotional vibration in which it returns to the table makes the exchange the more pathetic since nothing has happened. The Other who says he dwells in the others has not been received, and he has not taken unto himself this almsgiving self: that self continues to be a thief. "If I give everything I have to feed the poor, but have not love, I gain nothing."

As I delve into the gospel and venture into this area which attracts and terrifies me at the same time, I understand why Christ identified himself with the poor, with whoever has need of me. And I understand, too, why it is that "because you have done this to the least of my brothers, you have done it to me." The Other—the only liberator of my self, the only savior—is Christ. The sign that we have found him, that he has really liberated us, is that we shall have discovered the others and been received by them.

The career of Zacchaeus is the paradigm of the life of Charles de Foucauld. Rich, famous, enjoying life to the hilt, he too was one day struck by the thought of how tedious life had become. He felt imprisoned and unable to claw his way to freedom. The self without the Other is one-dimensional—like Zacchaeus climbing the tree to see the Other go by, not knowing who the Other is or what the Other requires of him. But as soon as Charles came to know the Other, the Other became an obsession with him; so much so that from that moment on, nothing apart from this Other held any interest for him. He was so fascinated that everything else became colorless. The decision to be poor, to abandon everything, was fundamentally a small thing because he had moved into a wholly new way of seeing things.

Certain amorous outpourings to the Beloved, which are not characteristic of him alone but of the mystics generally, can be a matter of debate. Freud attributes the phenomenon to a homosexual tendency. Nevertheless this passionate language has its source in this unique happening of life, not found in friendship or in sexual pleasure—which in itself is so often off-center—or in the pursuit of science, where the self is lost in an unending series of discoveries. The irreducibly Other is anterior to, it is closer than, sex; it is the humus of love, of friendship, of the scientific quest, of being among others. It is the condition through which I am among the others and for the others, instead of the others being for me.

The absolutely Other, the irreducibly Other, is certainly to be identified with the Son of Man, who has a history, a body, a human dimension and, naturally, a sex. Nevertheless, in this, his epiphany as liberator, he is presented as the Other, the foundation of all loves. It is an encounter which renews everything, brings everything to life and gives meaning to everything. All the words of love that we believed to be true become true. The Other that I have encountered is the true and profound meaning of love. I do not abandon everything in order to cling to him, because in him I discover the truth about all loves. And everything that is a projection of the self tumbles down, even though it might have the countenance and look of the other.

De Foucauld characterizes this period as a desire for silence, retreat, solitude. It is the wonder and bewilderment of the person unseated by the violent change in perspective. Perhaps it is the residue of the fear of the self which feels lost and experiences a need to solidify its defenses. Nevertheless, the encounter with the Other is the encounter with otherness, it is the liberation of the self, it is liberation and redemption because it is the winning of this capacity for new perspective. Charles de Foucauld was not long in discovering this new perspective.

In the Trappist monastery at Akbés one day they called upon him to take care of a sick man living in a hovel. From that moment on, he sees the monastery and sees himself, a Trappist—that is, an evangelical and penitential man—"from that hovel, from the miserable bed of the sick man, with his eyes." His brothers do not understand it, because the movement of "love" goes from the monastery to the village, whereas for Brother Albérico, as the convert was known in the monastery, it is going from the village to the monastery. It is not a question of someone going but of someone being received. The movement of Brother Albérico to the hovel is not real; what is real is the movement of welcome, of acceptance, on the part of the others. The Other silently cries out to him that he cannot be there or call himself brother and be so different, be from another rank, another class, another world.

Surely, those in the monastery have tried to talk him out of this with valid arguments and with all the subtle distinctions between poverty of spirit and sociological poverty. They have shown him the demands of the religious life, the protection needed for a life of prayer. But he is caught up in a new perspective. He does not see the others from the observation post of his self but from the observation post of the others. The Logos, the Word, Christ comes to view the Father from the perspective of human beings, and for this reason he has become compassionate. Saint Paul is impressed with this "emptying" of himself, which is not the charitable condescension of the rich but incarnation—that is, taking on in its reality the human condition.

Last year I spent a few days of Advent giving a retreat to a group of seminarians housed at a ranch outside Buenos Aires. The ranch property was subdivided and devoured by the flight from the country to the city. This has prodigiously extended the spread of the city. But what is left of the ranch is still there—the residence of the former owners, enormous compared to European estates. In the house a lovely group of nuns pray, cultivate splendid flowers, and give a warm welcome to people going there to pray.

The only thing that disturbs the serenity and the symphony of lines, of meadows, of gigantic trees, of the stream that courses artistically through the lawn and the rock garden, is the vulgar, miserable slum that surrounds the sacred walls. On one side the chants and the holy, childish joy of being together; on the other, the screams, the shouted threats, the off-key singing of drunks, the love songs, the screeching of children.

I tried to make the sisters understand that it might be well for a time to forego the traditional name of sister, because on one side of the wall it might make sense, but on the other it would make no sense, but provoke strong resentment. One of the sisters defended herself, telling me how much in debt to them those "on the other side of the wall" were. Did I not know how *many* of them knocked on their door, seeking alms? I was unable to make them understand that *love had a direction that is different from what they think.* "Make friends of them so that they will receive you," said Christ. And from the moment Christ settled on this meaning, we have been unable to change it. The sister will come to understand this only when she is able to view her mansion—where, as a spouse of Christ, she feels she has a perfect right to live her life protected from the filth of the world—from the slum, and only if she is able to see herself with the eyes of the slum-dweller. But this supposes liberation, the encounter with the Other. And it is by no means certain that all the piety, all the prostrations, all the long hours of prayer will be authentic encounters with the Other. As long as peace reigns there or as long as the sufferings amount to only the accursed torment of the self, the "good" sisters will go on without suspecting that the encounter with the Other is only a projection of the self. If they could at least have this doubt, perhaps out of it would come a hunger for otherness, which is the beginning of healing.

From Akbés, the itinerary of Father de Foucauld continues, sharpened by a mysterious hunger for the other. Since otherness is dynamic, it needs to be fed. It is a devouring fire that consumes. In the desert of Beni-Abbés, alone, without resources—the little help he gets from France is nothing more than a drop in the ocean, given the enormous poverty decimating the nomads. When the nomads pass by in their caravans or gather near the shelter of the hermit, Charles de Foucauld is overjoyed to learn that they have discovered his name—the name that has infinite resonances of delight for him: "brother." "They call me brother," he writes to a cousin. He is happy because he feels accepted, discovered, understood by the others. It is the sign that the Other has revealed himself to him, and otherness has become in him a sign of liberation. A history closer to our own and a personage not so much in the clouds can help us discover certain constants, certain laws. It is the history of the ordinary person, personified in Zacchaeus.

It is not enough to give alms—this can easily be a projection of the self. Giving everything away can be motivated by a sharpening of the need to atone, and for this reason it could be a decision, apparently heroic, to place the self on a very high pedestal.

Zacchaeus made a decision, looking at himself from the viewpoint of the others. "If I have defrauded anyone in the least, I will pay him back fourfold." He accepts the process that the crowd outside leads him to. He is not the rich man who, to celebrate the occasion, decides to give something he doesn't need to an orphanage in Jericho or to stuff the poor of the town with food for a day. No, he allows the others to tear the rich garments from him and to see him in his true poverty. The

wealthy publican, the chief tax collector, authorized and protected by the law, the man who has defended the right of the
strong, sees himself from the side of the others, of those who
make possible the privilege of the mighty. "You are not rich,
you are an exploiter."

I want to pin down one of the many images that strike me
when I read the gospel. The narrator, who does not ordinarily
get sidetracked, allows himself to dwell on one point. After
having noted the comment of the crowd, the judgment of the
people against Zacchaeus, he says: "Zacchaeus stood his
ground" (*stans, stathesis*), that is to say, neither whining nor
inflated with pride. This "standing his ground," apparently
adding nothing to the account (whose weight is centered on
the decision of Zacchaeus), tells me a lot. It tells me about the
courage, the serenity, the stability of someone who finds that
what the crowd is saying about him is perfectly normal and
logical. With firmness, without irritation—because everything
they say is objective—he decides with them and from their
point of view.

This perceptive observation about Zacchaeus, on the
psychological plane, is full of meaning. The mechanism of
guilt does not play a role here nor does atonement, the rather
dubious need for self-punishment. It is the logical discovery of
someone who *did not see* because he saw himself and the world
from the other side. Zacchaeus seen from the side of the others
is this and nothing more than this, and he is helpless to make a
decision other than the one that will make him "accepted" by
those whom he sees for the first time as the others. Liberation
has arrived, the liberator is the unique Other who called him
by his name on the road to Jericho; but the liberation becomes
history, becomes reality, through the others. The otherness
with which Christ has endowed him, freeing him from the
prison of his own self, becomes real with this judgment of the
people and the decision of Zacchaeus. They are the two complementary moments of the same liberation, so complementary that at times the Other, the only true liberator, disappears.

In the twenty-fifth chapter of Matthew, the "just"—those
who have come out of the self, those who have learned how to

love—will say with amazement, "When did we see you?" Because in reality they met with the others, with the people of this world who were hungry and thirsty, who were sick, in prison and homeless. The Other, through whom and in whom the others exist, remained hidden behind the others, in the mystery of the others. Love is not anonymous, it does not mean throwing money, and still less one's self, to be swallowed up in an abyss. To love is to meet with one who has a face and a name and who accepts me.

The Other, the one whom Zacchaeus went to see on the road to Jericho, is now his guest and, at the same time, the silent witness of the relationship that is being established between the owner of the house and the people. Zacchaeus turns all his aggressiveness into love, into acceptance, when he sees himself and his life from the viewpoint of those who have suffered injustice. And the Guest gives his stamp of approval to the event, pointing out that it has been the occasion for the grace of liberation. "Today salvation has come to this house." He does not give long sermons. This damnable foreigner has entered into the inheritance promised to the Chosen People because he has come out of himself and has found the Other.

The episode of Zacchaeus is a backdrop for all sermons on Christian hope and the forgiveness of sins. God is indulgent with us. He does not expect much of us—just a little tree-climbing.

In the gospel of Luke there is a constant revolutionary aspect that remains in the shadows: Salvation is given to the poor, the oppressed, those who suffer violence. And not in the sense that anonymous alms would balance scales unbalanced by the weight of injustice. The idea that God is offended, that God is unhappy with all the rotten things we do in life, is a concept that ought to be re-examined and reworked theologically because, as it stands, it is wrong. It generates the notion that God allows himself to be bribed like a government official. We have to put in order what is disordered through our sins, and this would seem to be an economic problem. We reject the idea that disorder is due to a self that is not liberated, blocked off in the infantile stage.

I do not believe it arbitrary to see the great episodes of history reduced to a matter of interpersonal relationships. One drop of blood tells the history of all bloodshed.

In this corner of Latin America that is not found on any map, I relive the history of Zacchaeus. Here the wounds have not healed, the wounds of Spanish colonialism, of English, and now American, imperialism and capitalism understood as economic exploitations which is the motive behind foreign domination in Latin America. A national pride, without roots because it is imported, has tried, in a stretch of history too brief for these peoples, to cover over the greed, the armed violence of the proud conquistadors, the insolent lack of respect toward civilizations that committed the one sin of remaining unarmed.

Here in this corner of America the poor continue to grind their corn on the perfectly round stones that the women of another era dug out of the rose-colored rock of the mountain. And they continue to build their huts out of cheap materials but with a perfection of line that would delight the greatest artists of the Renaissance. They close off their rooms with doors made almost entirely without tools, as artisans would have done in medieval Europe. (The cold crystal doors that open by photoelectric cells to let in, without the warmth of human welcome, the entrepreneurs who meet at the Sheraton or the Hilton are wholly lacking in this warm and harmonious beauty.) And their windows without glass—a material inaccessible to them because of distance and price—are closed with delicately worked shutters that took time, patience, and a harmony of spirit with which people who sacrifice beauty for comfort are unacquainted.

In this place I re-encounter human history, a history as hidden and tenacious as the roots of a plant or a weed mashed by the impatient hoe of someone clearing the land in order to dominate it.

These people, these creative poor to whom only beauty and humanity are left, are a silent indictment of the rich. With only the power of survival they point the finger at Zacchaeus and denounce him: "You are a thief, a sinful man." The rich have taken everything, and they continue to take the little that remains. But the more they take, the more they find themselves in a state of desperate loneliness, the more alien and hostile they become toward the others, the more they give up on them, the more they themselves become imprisoned in their one-dimensional lives, increasingly remote from the hour and from the possibility of liberation.

Many of those who present themselves as evangelists fail to evangelize because they have not discovered the "others" and have not courageously put themselves on the others' side. The only difference is that the evangelists look with pity, compassion, "benevolence" on those whom the rich and important people regard with arrogance, violence, and greed.

Jesus made a statement that has implications far beyond those of sexual morality: "What I say to you is: anyone who looks lustfully at a woman has already committed adultery with her in his thoughts" (Mt 5,28). Those who are adulterers in heart and desire, in perspective and look, are as much sinners as the adulterers in deed.

Now these peoples, these human communities, violated by power and force and looked upon with a *useless* compassion from the side of power and force, have in their hands what those responsible for colonialism, capitalism, and imperialism desperately need. They, these peoples, are the "others," the bearers of otherness.

All the religious who are busying themselves with consoling the rich and powerful in their desperate solitude, accompanying them into their frightening desert—these religious who are giving their lives to training the children of the rich in "mercy," "goodness," and "charity"—ought to be capable of one genuine act of love. It would be this: To let the "others" indict these rich people and thus reveal the true misery of Zacchaeus, let them point the finger at it and call it by its true name, now hidden under the nice-sounding term "welfare" or the very insulting term "protectionism." But the religious can do this only if they become "like the others." This supposes that they have been liberated, that they have lived and are living their encounter with the Other. It assumes that they are no longer "religious" in the sense of living in terms of bonds and formulas in easy fidelity to things and objects that are clear and well-defined, but are living in an I-Thou relationship of dialogue with this Other, who is exigent and disquieting, who is a devouring fire, and who does not rest until he has rooted out all the insidious ramifications of the self.

In *Populorum Progressio* there is hidden in the treatment of economic and political matters a prophetic indication that perhaps has not been sufficiently emphasized. There is certainly a complementariness between the rich nations and the poor, but it is not the kind of complementariness found when the first Europeans set foot in Latin America, sizing it up in terms of the magical twin words "capital" and "labor" with which priests and philosophers have always deceived us.

The liberation of the rich nations is in the hands of the poor nations. In this tragic hour of world history there is an urgent need for evangelizers who will at last look at the rich, the oppressors, with the gaze of the poor: *Only this can liberate them.* The poor will *never* be evangelized while they are looked upon with the eyes of the powerful, even though they are eyes full of pity, goodness, and sweetness. The rich will be evangelized only when they are looked upon with the eyes of the poor and denounced with that look, full of dignity and awareness of being truly "the others." All the decisions that might be made by those responsible for proclaiming Christ will be useless and self-defeating without this radical change of perspective, without the acceptance of the fact that the power of decision, the initiative of salvation, comes from the poor and the oppressed. Platonic sympathy and easy, superficial camaraderie are not enough to manifest this change; it is necessary to take upon oneself the history of the poor, their weariness, their quiet patience. It is necessary to discover in the ashes the precious things they have lost—their cultural values, their poetry; to hear again the voices suffocated by centuries of repression, their songs of pain and hope. It is necessary to accept the fact that the currents still flowing under the broken stones and the sands will rise again, breaking into a river threatening to sweep everything before it.

In his scornful invectives against the Pharisees, Jesus denounces the history of their plundering, their murder of the
prophets—all their evildoing under the varnish of justice and
religiosity.

As long as those who bear the responsibility for the proclamation of the gospel go on defining as "gentry" those who
hide oppression and violence behind phrases of understanding and compassion, making restitution of a tiny fraction
of the millions they have stolen, these evangelizers will betray
the poor and condemn the rich inexorably to their frightful
prison, to the desert of their incurable loneliness.

Jesus does not seek to pacify the accusers of Zacchaeus who
are making a disturbance at the door, nor does he make any
promises to them; he simply remains silent. He allows them to
make their judgment. Let the others, the liberators with all
their anger, invade the lonely life of the rich Zacchaeus. If he
has truly discovered the Other, really found out who He is and
come to know Him, he will evidence this by his ability to see
the others.

Marcuse, Koestler, Horkeimer, all those who find the
human condition desperate, seeing our culture, apparently in
a process of growth, shut in without an escape hatch, ought to
be reminded that only one person has said: "I am the door."
The world is without an escape hatch, and someone has said:
"I am the door." But so that we can be reminded, it is necessary that we should have discovered this door and passed
through it. The door does not lead to a vacuum, to what we call
the "transcendent": The transcendent has become immanent.
"I was hungry and you gave me to eat." This door leads to the
others, those who have a name, an identity, a history.

It is difficult to take a step toward the Other once we have
discovered the philosophical barricades (the hardest to vault)
for guaranteeing the security of the self and closing off the
entrance. We have been convinced that the "out there," the
"beyond," the "other" do not exist. The caricatures of dualism
and a theatrical transcendence have been used to condemn us
to dig within ourselves interminable tunnels that are our space
and time. Whereas space and time are not ours; they "are" the

"others." The gospel speaks of human beings as ones who are to be received. Just as other phrases have been coined to describe human beings—*homo politicus, homo oeconomicus*—I would like to coin the phrase "person born to be accepted," the "acceptable," acceptable to the Other in order to be acceptable to the others.

Christ is not just one more of the many escape hatches, one of the safety valves of the self. He is the only door, the only way, the only Other. And it is necessary to present him in this way, violently. All the patches that we could put on the torn garment of Christian civilization do no more than widen the rent. We should look upon Christian civilization from the point of view of the other civilizations that it has rejected, snuffed out, and denied. In the midst of these ruins of civilization, covered with earth and ashes, the Other has remained, because as Saint Paul would say, "What of it? All that matters is that in any and every way, whether from specious motives or genuine ones, Christ is being proclaimed! That is what brings me joy. Indeed, I shall continue to rejoice" (Phil 1,18).

And these are the others from whose point of view we must see our Christian civilization with its alignment with colonialism, capitalism, and imperialism—three narcissistic, ego-worshiping phenomena fixed in the anal phase of our human evolution. Perhaps the highest courage asked of us is to remain silent to allow the others to indict our manner of life. What can save us and the world is the wrath of the poor, just as the wrath of those gathered around the house of Zacchaeus rescued the publican from his loneliness.

Evangelization is not done so much with words, with a doctrinal content that the poor do not understand and suspect as being a trap. To evangelize is to shed light on the event of liberation that Christ has accomplished, and that is all. The others have succeeded in unblocking an individual from his loneliness. Finally someone has acquired sight, hearing, movement, has begun to see and be aware of the others, to walk toward them and with them. This is the clear and evident sign that the irreducible Other, who is more intimate than our own self because he goes much deeper, has been accepted.

"Today salvation has come to this house." Only those who have accepted the Other can be evangelists, because they are capable of discerning the coming and the acceptance of the absolute "Thou," wherever he may have come from and in whatever way he has been accepted. As long as we have not accepted the Other, we will defend ourselves with theories elaborated by the self to preserve its wretched self-contemplation.

"Capitalism is certainly to be condemned, but I know a lot of fine capitalists." "Today colonialism is unthinkable, but at least you can say that it opened up the road to progress, civilization, and the gospel." Theologians do not have to be nudged to find distinctions: "There is no reason to be radical. Be more precise in your thinking." Surely Jesus knew Pharisees who were very fine people. Let us imagine that someone might have tugged at his sleeve while he was delivering his string of curses and said: "Take it easy. At least make it clear which Pharisees you are talking about. Exclude those who have invited you to lunch, clarify carefully the difference between ideology and the person. Specify that what you are talking about is a matter for justifiable anger, not hatred." But Jesus holds nothing back; his prophetic rage is strongly rooted in firm ground: the despoiled widow, the man bent under an intolerable burden, the young men won for the kingdom after an astute and tenacious siege and afterwards perverted by the bad example of the "teachers," the bloodstains of the stoned prophets, the invited guests put in the lowest place or pushed to the side of the road to make way for the proud and contented "gentlemen." From that ground he cries out to them from the depth of the love they have scorned, and his cry is an invitation to liberation for all, great and small.

Those who are in charge of evangelizing often appeal to charity, to sensitivity, to humility, in order not to abandon their position. If they could but find the Other and go with him to the other side, they would be ashamed of their excuses and of their recriminations, which hide a real lack of love.

A religious friend of whom I am very fond was telling me simply and good-naturedly that the splendid Alfa Romeo parked at his door was not driven by a benefactress but by a miserable woman who had come seeking his advice on how to get out of a tough situation.

But, my dear brother, we are going to have to close our counselling offices, for they are attracting fewer and fewer clients, thus leaving the field to the psychoanalysts. We are not the ones who can free these slaves. We do not have the tools necessary to open their prison doors. Certainly we can say that Christ exists, that he is the Consoler, the Other, and distribute itineraries and point out the road. But do we by any chance have the courage to open the window and let the cry of the poor enter—Murderer! Thief!—so that the one who has come for counselling can hear it, the one who comes in anguish over a betrayal, a disillusionment, a non-love? Do we have this kind of courage?

Jesus uses two different methods. In the case of Zacchaeus—powerful, rich, broken by the torment of his loneliness—he opens the window so that his host can hear the accusatory comment of the crowd, even if he himself is involved in the accusation for having gone out of his way to visit the house of a sinner. In the square where they are about to stone the adulteress, he takes a threatening stance toward the "wise," those who are accusing her and want to stone her, and disperses them. The two different approaches have an undeniable coherence because they arise from the same point of view. It is a question of seeing the happening from the side of the oppressed, of those who are beaten down by wealth, power, and a paternalism that hides its oppression under the cloak of righteousness.

The anguish of the lady who drives the red Alfa Romeo, my brother, neither you nor I will ever mitigate. A political overthrow, the rising of the poor to power—will this rid the world of that anguish, that human suffering, which the rich bring, in an Alfa Romeo or in a private jet, to the specialists in pain-killing? I don't think anyone believes this, least of all those who give their lives for a change in structures, confident that thus will begin the age of the new person. But can we pretend to clarify or resolve these dramas of the human spirit—which are variants of the one drama—without going into otherness, without "the others"?

Whatever we could say to the lady with the red automobile in her real anguish would help extend the space of her self, imprisoned behind bars that close in ever more tightly as the physical spaces available to her become wider. What should we, responsible for proclaiming the gospel, say if we see that the true liberators—those who really love the rich, the lady with the Alfa Romeo and the oil, copper, and banana barons —are those who bring to the surface of history the cry of the oppressed, and, without a lot of "distinctions," denounce the three diabolical structures that bar the self from the others and the others from the self, closing the door to the Other: colonialism, capitalism, and imperialism—which is to say wealth, possession, and power? The three dimensions of the person, the three roads to relationship, of access to the others, are sealed off by the unscalable walls the self has built to defend itself.

There is but one sorrow in the world. "To his own he came, yet his own did not accept him" (Jn 1,11). "Here is the one who will inherit everything. Let us kill him" (Mt 21,38). Our deep sadness is to be found in the look of Christ when he saw the rich man go away—after he had come with such enthusiasm in his Alfa Romeo and was hoping to solve his problem between the two of them, without the others intruding. Instead, the others do intrude: "Go and sell what you have and give to the poor; you will then have treasure in heaven. After that, come and follow me" (Mk 10,21).

So that the Other will not be an idol, which would be repugnant, the others must decide. If they receive him, if they are friends, it is because he has found the Other. Crises cannot be solved by one-to-one counselling sessions; not even a miracle-worker is of any help; there is need of the intervention of the others, who are a reflection—the human presence—of the irreducible Other.

This presumed charity is not true charity. The radicalization of Pasolini—who leaves us crying out in the desert—is closer to love, to the revelation of the Other, than the easy, smiling abstract counsel with which, like an endorsement, we try to compromise Christ, Christ made in our own image.

There is no salvation other than that of discovering that our only misfortune is genuine loneliness—not that which is seen, but the interior loneliness that congeals the self and makes it inaccessible to any other person or any other love. If this unhappy lady, alone and without the irreducible Other, does not liberate herself from complicity in and responsibility for the gigantic structures which are a defensive and aggressive projection of the self, all that we can give her are temporary sedatives. The sermon that Jesus preaches to Zacchaeus is simply this: "You are unhappy because you are alone; you are alone because you are a sinner; and you are a sinner because your aggressive and unaccepting life prevents others from receiving you." This is the real drama of the one-dimensional person.

The church senses this, yet many of its structures are made in the image of the squalid structures of the self. They are not evangelical. We are the proclaimers of a word that was announced within a certain perspective, from a definite direction. This word has become a chorus and been transformed into a saving threat because it is an invitation that comes from the others, from those we long for with tears and groans but who reject us.

Many of the words and threats of the gospel sound false and ineffectual if we fail to think of the platform and the community from which and within which Christ pronounced them. It is a perspective that gives life and veracity to the gospel and makes it efficacious for all generations and in all desperate cases. And those of us who are responsible for repeating it in time and space should see it this way and in this way make it our own.

5

The Adventure of Freedom

. . . because this son of mine was dead and has come back to life. He was lost and is found. Then the celebration began (Lk 15,24).

In the account of the prodigal son, the thematic lines of the message are clear: conversion as discovery of the possibility of being lost and the unshakable will to salvation; anti-Phariseeism as opposition to the "acquired right," to a blood inheritance; sympathy toward those who are able to change —those who "open a hole in the roof," tug at the sleeve of his garment, climb a tree—as opposed to the static pride of those who take no initiatives because they see themselves as within their rights. But the account, which is profoundly human, expresses much more than our right to hope.

Nothing is said about the mother, who would certainly be affected emotionally by the return; it is, after all, a story of the break with an outgrown identity and discovery of a new one. The boy got along well with his father; he identified comfortably with him. The memory of his father's house is not obscured by any recollection of severity or rejection: "How many hired hands at my father's place have more than enough to eat while here I am starving!"

Why did he leave home? His leaving is the affirmation of the self determined to get out from under his father, to be someone, to gain his freedom independently of the father. Today, with the understanding we now have, this does not seem to be an unjust demand: "Father, give me the share of the estate that is coming to me." And we find the wordless response of the father normal and right: "So the father divided up the property."

But if we make fatherhood out to be a static dependence, a relationship into which we are born, unchangeable through time, the request of the young man seems like open rebellion. The silence of the father, in this view, would seem to be the silence of a weak and undecided man, of a man who does not love because he cannot. However, the silence is that of normality. Why doesn't the father hold on to the son, why doesn't he make him wait, why doesn't he give him a slap on the head instead of the "share of the estate that is coming to him"? Because the gospel gives us the lines of normality, and not a false sentimentalism or cheap apologies. It does not put forth arguments to defend a pathological paternalism that suffocates the growth of the other.

It is a new story that begins. And it begins always in this way, with the "dis-identification" with the father who is, unconsciously, the mold in which the son has been formed. Taken objectively, the act is not sinful or rebellious; it is an act of courage. One form of moralistic interpretation would stress the son's asking for "the share of the estate that is coming to me" as an act of disloyalty and rebellion. If God is Lord and Creator, nothing is "coming to us." Not so. The Creator does not keep the world for himself, granting ungraciously a few crumbs that we grab from his hand, like workers worming a few rights out of the boss. This is a pagan concept, not a Christian one. We can find no analogy in the Bible for Prometheus, who "steals" the secret of the gods. "With the coming of Christ, the world has achieved such a radical form in its secularity, has become so *atheist*, that man today, on the sheer strength of this coming, can face the world without recourse to other gods in order to understand it" (J.B. Metz, *Sulla teologia del mondo*, p. 61).

Because we exist the world belongs to us, the world is ours. We have displaced the center of adoration, of relationship with God, *from being to having* (where *doesn't* the cursed economic view assert itself?). We feel that we are beggars, strangers in the world, and God seems to be a despot, an idol who doles things out capriciously. I have noticed that the rich are always saying that they are mere administrators and not owners; they are quick to say: "You can't take it with you," "We have to leave it all behind." This seems to be a humble posture. In fact, they continually revive the "divine right of kings." They see themselves as "the vicars, the administrators of God," and this is not exactly humility.

To exist means to be and to communicate with things. The mature and unresentful silence of the father I find convincing. Perhaps he is saddened that the great adventure is about to start—there is ambiguity here—but he is not angered by the demand. The view of a despotic father who has absolute ownership over all goods has formed in us an erroneous conscience which is partly responsible for the pathological use we make of things.

The boy emerges from a life that had no definition other than that determined by the father. *Eros* awakens him from his state of passivity. He sees his own value and the need to possess. Psychoanalysis has investigated this mysterious awakening of youth and has made very important discoveries, even when they are somewhat lost in the mythology that tries to explain the birth of the person and of a culture. The gospel of Luke is particularly aware of this "awakening," the liberation of youth. The childhood of Christ himself culminates in the episode of the rupture with the family on the occasion of the journey to Jerusalem. The relationship with the father is a rediscovery after the rupture, a conscious option rather than a passive acceptance of an original state. I do not see a rebellion here but an awakening of responsibility. The drama comes later. The choice is realized "in a distant country"; love ends in loneliness, relationship with goods in poverty; his status is lowered by his working as a peasant taking care of pigs.

All the pathos of fatherhood is to be found in this experience of seeing what the young choose and seeing where it will end—seeing not with an indifferent curiosity but with a painful attention, with a suffering become incarnate. The father in

Luke does not go with the son; he lets him go. His silence can be interpreted in ways that are most contradictory. It can be thought that he remained angry, offended. I like to think he remained expectant, hoping. Goods are to be given; the journey must be made; he cannot substitute himself for the choice of the son.

The gospel seems pessimistic. It would seem to give us to understand that the man in a "distant country" is fated to ruin himself in the use of his autonomy and liberty. Worldwide alienation, the situation wherein we live which prevents us from being "ourselves" authentically, is certainly the projection of people who have destroyed themselves, who have not known how to make their options wisely. We should conclude, as does Koestler, that we are a demented race: Our course is now full of anxiety because of the fear of atomic destruction.

I would like to talk about a modern version, one I have lived through, of the fifteenth chapter of Luke. The girl: beautiful, intelligent, highly endowed, sensitive, and intuitive. She was capable of penetrating into the meaning of things so profoundly that she seemed to have a superhuman power. She was able to grasp instantly and totally a film, a page from the Bible, a happening, the mystery of a person; she could see things in a glance that I could scarcely manage to perceive fragmentarily after a tiring intellectual search. I don't know by what intuitive process I was able to discover in her signs of neurosis: a lack of authenticity, an evident imbalance between lucidity of intuition and passivity and inertia in getting to work—as if all her energy were concentrated on the process of intuition, leaving empty the moment for action. Every so often, in unexpected flare-ups, her superego, her narcissism, would appear. Her generosity, her altruism, which led her to give away things of great value and to lend unstinting help to others, would emit, from time to time, the signal of a devouring egocentricity. The "other" for whom she sacrificed whatever she had and for whom she "handed over her body to be burned" was really her self, her self disguised under the appearances of the other. The boy: graduate in medicine with psychiatry as his specialty, a brilliant mind, outgoing, altruistic, apparently well-balanced. They came to know each other in our community during a dramatic moment of the Algerian War. They were both serving in the army. It became necessary to share ideas, identify emotions, shed light on the interchange—a frightfully ambiguous situation. Thus began a friendship that matured rapidly, transforming itself into love. I had the feeling that there would never be a true union because of a radical psychic impotence. But he was a psychiatric intern in the clinic; he told himself that he was thoroughly aware of her pyschic weaknesses. In his judgment they complemented each other perfectly. He was the man for her, the only one who could have gotten her out of the swamp into which she was inexorably sinking. I well remember that when I greeted them at that harbor in Africa from which they were leaving to get married, I felt the need to make one more attempt to get them to think it over.

Six years later, I received a mysterious letter with an invitation. As soon as I got the opportunity to go to that city on the coast of France, I hastened to the house of my friends. I found them completely unstrung. Never have I had more direct evidence, a clearer picture, of the destruction of a person. A series of complications, of real or imaginary commitments, was obliging them to stay together. Now the reason for living was that of destroying one another little by little. She in her delirium had burned all her husband's notes; the fruits of his time-consuming studies, his bibliography, the outlines of papers to be done. He had not known how to objectify this behavior and see it in its pathological configuration; he lacked the courage to remake his existence. The only delight left in his life was to take vengeance. Because of this—or perhaps out of sheer impotence—they were unable to make the decision to separate, like the tragic couples of Beckett, buried in sand or lost among the refuse of the garbage heap or rolling around, as slippery as worms, in a strange cylinder that never stops turning.

The mystery of the option has always tormented me. Without making a free choice one cannot live. And I have the impression that people make their decisions under a weak and tenuous light, spurred on by an immense and brutal passion. If this break with the father does not come about, this disidentification, adulthood will never come. Is revolt, rebellion, necessary? Maybe not; but the break, yes.

The adolescence of Christ is transmitted to us under no other sign but this, a profoundly human and normal sign. It has taken the whole personalist experience and all the research into depth psychology for us to discover in this break a psychological law, a law that has no moral significance. Without this finding it had been difficult to accept in the Holy Family a dialectic element, an affective tension that Luke talks about so simply in the second chapter of his gospel. The young man is obeying a law that arises from his time of life. I ask myself to what point the father could be of help to his son through his experience, his counsel—the father who *must be rejected* with this decision, the father who is the terminus of the parting, not just the "topographical place" but the "existential, psychological place."

Until we face love in all its forms with this lack of prejudice, we will never come to understand it, and we will remain enclosed in the sphere of superficial and tepid romance. We are inheritors of the kind of thinking in which love and friendship exist and their joys and advantages are described for us. Cicero and Seneca are models, and our Christian literature follows rather dutifully in their paths. It is true that artistic creations have always broken these molds and shown us that things are not always as they are pictured, but our little sermons do not differ much from humanistic literature. Love, whatever its form, requires absolute *freedom*, and without it there can be no love. If the son had not "rejected" the father, and if the father had not resigned himself to being "rejected," would this free choice to love have existed?

This is the point that ought to be pondered by all those who *demand* to be loved as if they were demanding a right. ("I'm your father! It's the last straw for you not to love me!" God never says to his creatures: "I have created you; I've given you everything, including your life. It's all I need, that you should not love me!") It should be pondered by those, too, who try to obtain love by giving a false picture of themselves. Thus, just as they fail to respect the unique freedom in the gift of the other, so they get nothing in return but the echo of their own maneuver. They are condemned to seeing themselves frustrated in the very thing they are demanding—union in total freedom. Here we have a tremendous and truly sacrificial mystery. (P. Roqueplo, *Expérience du monde: expérience de Dieu?*)

A friend or a group of friends would have been able to help the son, but not the father. If we do not want to go on being children, we must venture into the "hostile universe" and face the risk of ruin—of encountering people and events which, instead of freeing us, will bring about our "perdition." And just what is the road to salvation and what is the road to perdition? A life that moves gradually upward, one in which everything is as symmetrical as in a game of chess, sometimes ends in a swamp. Schooling, military service, marriage—all are such well-calculated and synchronized movements that life arrives at its epilogue smoothly and victoriously. However, a ruined life can end up in reconstruction, in an unforeseen greatness.

Christ has completely changed the plans of the Pharisees. They were trying to wrap life up in the law. The pharisee of today cannot resist the temptation to manipulate life with all the calculations of foresight; but then it is no longer human life, it is a life for chickens. It seems to us that a life which, owing to its harmony and its lack of dialectical tensions, keeps us in a blessed infantilism—we are satisfied with ourselves and able to pass on to our descendants, along with our hoarded capital, our accumulated boredom—is more "ruined" than an ardent, expended life which expresses a person's total capacity for love, notwithstanding the irregularity of the game and the enormous ambiguity of the options.

The gospel tells us in a thousand ways that the important thing is not to "win," but to arrive at the discovery of the other. And in this context the silence of the father, his profound respect for the son who is facing a "hostile world," seems right. We have always read the Good News from a moralistic perspective, even when there is no certainty that the moral is there, and we have thus not seen the fullness of the human riches it contains. Certainly the alternative between the infantile life and the ruined life is false. There are people who find themselves in the epilogue of their life full of the joy of living and not regretting their past, people who have become adults, maturing through the options and through the love that bring security to the others. There are people who have arrived at a peace distinct from that of the tomb, who have achieved the capacity for living without guilt complexes or pathological tangles—a capacity for accepting things as they are. In what way, by what grace, have these people come to grasp life, with its possibility of synthesis, confronting the ruptures and options without destroying themselves? Certainly not without undergoing "death," not without accepting a kind of destruction, for the capacity for loving people, life, nature, history, is a "moderation" that does not come naturally to flesh and blood. This is the new vision, mind, capacity that Paul speaks of, attributing this transformation to the resurrection.

In the context of the gospel, God does not appear like the father who locks the door so that the children cannot go out at night. Rather, God is like a light on our way, like a compass guiding us in our options, someone who does not abandon us in the risky exercise of freedom but who creates new horizons for liberation, refashioning epilogues that seemed headed for disaster. The father can help only by being a detached model, if it can be put that way; and for this reason he must accept being "destroyed as model."

There are present in the gospel two models of fatherhood. One of them ought to be smashed and abandoned: the fatherhood that transmits life to us laden with the dead weight of heritage—the archaic fears, the commitment to power, which is the terrible nemesis of history. The other fatherhood is to be achieved and coincides with the discovery of our identity. The adventure of the prodigal son ends well not because it goes from moral decadence to recovered dignity but because it goes from a "non-meaning" to a "meaning." All the stages from the departure to the return are redeemed by the embrace of the father. The return to the house of the father is the rediscovery of the meaning of things and events. First there is the non-meaning of unawareness, the non-meaning of one who has not been freed from dependency and therefore has not been tested by concrete options. The journey of the son is a quest for an awareness of the love that envelops him without his realizing it and which gives him only feelings of comfort and boredom.

We have not thought enough about the distinction between the fatherhood that is the "terminus from which one leaves," *terminus a quo,* and the fatherhood that is the "terminus at which one arrives," *terminus ad quem.* The resulting confusion causes many mistakes and seems to authorize a father-son relationship that is highly infantile. Some who are reading this will think the above is just too much, because, in their view, the love of God is given without our self-denial, it can be discovered without break-offs. Their trouble is that they have never reflected, until now, on the mystical experience, which is the only experience of God; they rely on a "religious experience" of the law, of ritual, of *praxis.* An experience of God unavoidably undergoes negation: Jesus' "My God, my God, why have you forsaken me?"; the experience of Job, "I cry to you, but you do not answer me; you stand off and look at me" (Job 30,20). It is necessary to break off dependency in order truly to discover oneself in the real world. To discover God as the *other distinct from self, and not a projection of self,* there is no other way but to discover the self as the "other distinct from God." The dark nights of the mystics have nothing to do with the childish game of hide-and-seek; they tell of an experience of being "separate," distinct, without relationship.

Luke's account is a kind of digest: the departure, ruin, and return follow each other in quick succession; but we can actually imagine a long space of time between the different moments of the venture. The son does not return to the father to escape the phantasms of a hostile world; it is a return to reality, to identity. He is stripped of the alienating factor of his money. He thinks about those who work in his father's house and asks to be a part of this group. The father restores his dignity; he puts him back into his history, into his identity. But nowhere does it say that he restores his lost goods. The relation of the youth to his goods seems turned around. Before, his goods followed him, went with him—he carried his inheritance in his pockets. Afterwards, it is he who goes toward the goods. They are in front of him and against him as a challenge he must accept and resolve through work. The father reassures the elder "capitalist" brother, worried by the fear of losing something. He tells him, "You are with me always, and everything I have is yours." You will lose nothing. Just let me celebrate the homecoming party.

The prodigal had to have this experience of losing everything that was alienating him, preventing him from experiencing the real, in order to find himself again, identifying himself and thus discovering a liberated and liberating love. Before the journey, the son was not "other" to the father, and thus fatherhood would seem to be truly a drama, because it is not a static, permanent relationship. At a certain point it should change from being "physiologically" creative to "psychically" creative—personalist—and this change brings about a dying in which the stalk of the flower, the tree-trunk, the continuation of the father-self, becomes really the thou, the other.

In our Christian jargon "responsible parenthood" most of the time means non-creative parenthood. Responsible signifies, in the language of Christian movements, to make the relationship center on the father and thus give it pretensions, weight, power. Liberation consists precisely in the reduction of this power.

The view of a naive and escapist anthropology, originating in the heady atmosphere of the first discoveries of psychoanalysis, presented the schema of life—the passage from the undefined to the individual—in the myth of the father's death or his being reduced to impotency by the children, egged on by blind and violent jealousy. Under the myth we discover that it is the son who brings about liberation, not the father. The new fatherhood, the new relationship, is not a decision the father makes after returning from a seminar; it is the decision of the son. We should speak of a "responsible sonship." We can speak to fathers about responsible fatherhood as acceptance of their limitations, of this "disappearance." "It is necessary that he grow and that I diminish." As always it is the poor, the oppressed, who take the initiative toward liberation. It would probably scandalize a lot of people to talk of fatherhood as a kind of oppression, to designate as a relationship of oppression what is a relationship of love, care, and concern. Nevertheless, from a certain angle fatherhood is oppression because it keeps the person in the phase of indeterminateness—in what Paul Ricoeur, translating Freud, calls the *ça* (the "that"). It prevents the individual from awakening, from standing erect as a person, the only one capable of shaping his life.

The Bible speaks of creation and re-creation, of birth and rebirth, of a fatherhood to reject and one to choose. Creation is a movement that goes from the father to the son; re-creation, one that goes from the son to the father. Fatherhood of the flesh is given us; that of the spirit is chosen. To discover the father is to discover the whole series of happenings lived in a dialectic which issues in the creation of the individual. It is like going back to the beginning, and from that point looking back over the road that has been travelled, discovering in it a positive and creative wholeness, seeing it as life.

I consider Paul's thought a fathomless depth when he refers to Christ as the one who "restores all things to the Father at the end." This cannot be interpreted as a restitution of things taken on loan, a payment to the owner; it must be seen as a reunification of all things, as the "oneness of meaning" that all things—all events, "good or evil"—have taken on through the creative and salvific presence of Christ, through his mediation. The life-project of the Son has made of the reality dispersed in time a marvelous synthesis which is his paschal life, the life of the resurrection. Entering into this life through his union with the Other, the person who had gone astray in things returns to that point of departure where life is a seed—that is, a unit. It is the return from plurality. It is an emergence in which all things are caught up and none is rejected, inasmuch as all things enter into the creation or the re-creation of the self that is emerging.

After reflecting on the text of Luke an image of conversion occurs to me. The concept of conversion also is quite deformed in our Christian culture. Conversion means a change of attitude, a change of viewpoint. But it is also a passing from an ego that feels dirty and mired in sin to a superego, that is, a passing from a "lost ego," perplexed over the realization of itself as design, to a *false* ego. Nothing much is gained. There the "convert" oscillates between self-exaltation and depression, between childishness and bold statements, because this pseudoconversion consists in taking off wolf's clothing in order to dress in sheep's clothing. Clothing at all costs, something that is not one's own. True conversion is that which brings us back to reality. It is to discover and to accept from the heart what we are. For this reason conversion in the gospel is often represented as an opening of the eyes, as a seeing. Without warning, this little disordered, incoherent thing that is our life is penetrated by a great and mysterious love, by a "concern" that is not in us but in the Other.

The young man could have punished himself after having discovered that he had not loved his father and that he had misspent his life. Why not accept a life of expiation among the pigs which would have made him the founder of armies of penitents? No, he returns to his father's house to be that which he is, stripped of his childish illusions and of the grand design of the superego. He becomes a creature again, but with the awareness of being one. The father has nothing to give him but the signs of his identity: that he is one of the family, that he is the one who left, who died and now has risen from the dead. He does not tell the elder son to set up a little place for him out in the vineyard, or to give the boy some of his cattle because "everyone has a right to a living." No, the party is an interval of joy over the birth of a person. From the sad breakaway, from ruin in a hostile world, from the loss of property, there emerges a man who "was lost and has been found, dead and risen again."

While I am writing these lines, the radio is blaring forth a gross commercial, comparable only to the Coca-Cola commercials, for a slim North American novel, *Love Story*, which is one more of many translations of the parable, camouflaged with a frank account of a love affair. This "biography of man" has tempted many artists. From the great adventure story of N'toni, hero of Sicilian literature, to the trivialities of the Harvard student, and going on to the enormous challenge of *The Grand Inquisitor* of Dostoyevsky, the "temptation of freedom" is seen as constitutive of the human being. But the colorless North American novel was evidently inspired by a nocturnal conversation after Wall Street had closed its offices. This explains in part the disproportionate amount of publicity that has been given the book. It is the youth rebellion seen from the side of the parents. It rings false. As a love story it is every bit as insipid as the roseate novels of the turn of the century. As a biography of youth, as a "story of the adventure of freedom," it is not true. It tries to empty the youth rebellion of all its prophetic value and of its revolutionary freight, robbing the crisis of its impact. The point it attempts to make is this: the crisis of youth is merely the crisis of eroticism. Wink at, be indulgent toward the erotic, affective, sentimental escapades and you will have a young man who will end up in the arms of his father. Obviously the intention of patriarchal society is to control, direct, and organize the crisis from beginning to end.

The gospel speaks of someone who is *dead, ruined.* Let us not smooth over these strong and realistic words. It was necessary that the "power," "worth," and "possession"—that is, the personality and the history—of the father should become really his, pass into his hands and through this crisis of destruction and death, so that he, the son, could become "other." The end of *possession* takes place because he squanders his wealth; of *worth*, because from being the son of a rich man he goes on to be a tender of pigs; of *power*, because no one receives him and he finds himself in a frightening loneliness. Undergoing this reduction to impotence is the one condition on which the three constitutive structural elements of the person—power, worth, possession—can be interiorized, can become factors of awareness instead of instruments of the person.

Speaking of Christ the miracle-worker, the evangelist says

that power went forth from him. And this power frees, personifies, gives the word; whereas power in general enslaves, "thingifies." The power of Christ is identified with the person; from "external power," "power in the aggregate," it becomes a structural force, unifying itself in the person. This power of Christ has also undergone an emptying out, the crisis of total poverty: "He emptied himself and took the form of a slave, being born in the likeness of men" (Phil 2,7). The text is rich in meaning. If Christ had come into the world with the power of the Father (from the Father to the Son), it would not really have raised him up, liberated him, re-created him. Liberation, re-creation, goes from the son to the father. And it is necessary that the life of the father—which is power, worth, possession —should be *renounced*. He annihilated himself, killed off his life. I never tire of the richness of this text. Note the preceding verse: "Though he was in the form of God, he did not deem equality with God something to be grasped at. Rather, he emptied himself" (Phil 2,6).

To place the prodigal son and Christ side by side seems blasphemous, and yet Paul says that in this emptying of himself, in this "destruction," Christ was born in our likeness, he became like us. We arrive at the emptying of ourselves through sin, whereas Christ achieved it through love. In our case, it is experience and things that empty us, whereas in the story of the Incarnation it is love that impels Christ to empty himself in order to take on his manhood. The Father creates (movement of the Father to creation, a movement that is a display of the power, worth, and possession of the Father). The Son re-creates; that is, he takes on creation from within (the movement of the Son to the Father which is a matter of renouncing the power, worth, and possession of the Father).

N'toni, the protagonist of Verga's novel, is not a socialite from the New York suburbs, but he is profoundly authentic. On his return home after his journey to freedom, he says, "Now I know, now I see that I have to go." His sister tries to show him that nothing has changed, that everything is still in place. But he feels that the things he has left have entered into him, they are his conscience, his conscious self, and therefore do not belong to him. For this reason he must leave. His grandfather's things no longer are his; he has killed them off, and they have become changed into his experience, his way of being human.

N'toni Malavoglia knows that he must go because he has ceased to lean on his father. When things go up in smoke they enter into his history. He returns home to touch his identity, to find himself again among the persons and things he grew up with. He is N'toni Malavoglia, born in a Sicilian village amid barrels of sardines in a house surrounded by the murmur of the sea. He still sees the shadow of his mother on the chairs. He is the same and yet he is other; he feels he must pinch himself to see if he still is himself, so strange has he become since his bolt to freedom. The poetry of the last page of *Malavoglia* is centered on the long look he casts on things in the house, feeling that he is in communion with them and yet a stranger to them, that they belong to him and yet they don't. It is as though he were rediscovering them after having died, looking at them from "within himself" because he can no longer see them from "within the father."

We can live our whole life alienated within the power, worth, and possession of the father, in a kind of a comfortable casing in which we were born. And this is the highest treason that the middle-class family wreaks upon the children. The price that the rich man immediately pays for the goods he has squirreled away, in prejudice to others, is this: the possibility of leaving an inheritance to his children that will close off the road of life for them. Through a strange irony the rich man accumulates money on the pretext of "opening up the road" for his children and in reality he does just the opposite. The truth is that breaking away from this alienation means entering into another alienation—to lose oneself, to squander oneself, until one is alone, reduced to emptiness, to essential nakedness, to impotency. And this emptying of self, this clearing away of the brushwood suffocating us so that we can find ourself, how do we do this?

The adventure into awareness is a terrifying and difficult adventure. It passes necessarily through the cross and death.

It is the human adventure. Without these vicissitudes we are not human. We keep on living because physiology never goes on strike, but physiology is not the person. And it is not only the adventure of the children; it is also that of the parents, the recreation of parenthood. Parenthood loses its identity of origin. The father is no longer "he who gives" but "he who receives in restitution," as Paul might say. Father and son are now adults: Between them there is no longer power and possession, they are two poor men, two free men. The discourse of the father to the older son is a psychological master-stroke: "Have no fear, I have no intention of changing anything, everything will remain in its place." The younger brother is not coming to demand anything; he is coming to find himself, to feel reborn, and he had no other place to find himself except here, where his identity began.

The parable is the story of all of us. The crisis, the rupture, is not a phenomenon confined to one epoch; it is the psychological law of all. Only by undergoing this breaking away through which the son is changed into "other" does parenthood become a genuine relationship, a "parenthood restored," that is, chosen. Parenthood is not a static value to which one has a right because of an age difference. It is a value that must be sought after, earned. If the adult generation could only understand this, how the world would be transformed! This is the eternal problem: Each of us is ready to be burned alive, but none of us is ready to "receive the other." It is the problem of authority, of age, of power. It is the problem of the world of the "publicans" and the "pharisees," that is, of the "rich" in worth, power, and possession face-to-face with the challenge of Christ.

The patriarchal society is justly indicted. Nevertheless parenthood is extolled in the gospel to the point that we can call the gospel the "message of the father." But if we do not clear up the misunderstanding, if we do not see parenthood "after the rupture," "after the death," "after the resurrection," we run the risk of extolling the kind of parenthood that the gospel radically denies. In the second chapter of Luke, the silence of Mary is worthy of note. She does not understand;

she is hurt, but "she kept all these things in memory." It is the moment in which motherhood is reconstructed, is born of the rupture that occurs in the son's adolescence.

The tension of our age is more evident than in the past; perhaps because we have much more of everything, the load of guilt has become heavier. The crisis is not to be resolved with admonitions or decisions of the will: Ours is a culture that must die. Afterwards it will be reborn, but it cannot be corrected, modified; it must be destroyed.

The young generation is discovering the human person, his qualitative growth, and wants to destroy savagely anything that threatens to stand in the way of their breakthrough—the church, society, the family, that is, all those who have "experience," who know where things will end up. The generation of the fathers has discovered wealth and the laws to multiply it—quantitive growth. There can be no meeting of the minds; the two generations speak different languages. Which one should die? I would say the two of them. The young generation should die the "death of risk"; the renunciation of security, stability, of a warm womb in which to mature and live. The adult generation should give up on providing security, stability—in a word, certainty; it should renounce its wealth. The return of the son, from this perspective, could be an encounter between two poor men. If we do not accept the crisis but pretend to be getting it under control or patching things up, we will hold back the coming of the new world. And it is time it came, because the old world is becoming more and more chilled by the terror of collective self-destruction. In accepting the crisis, in spite of all the unknowns that arise, we will bring about the cleansing of our desire. From economic ambition we will go on to the desire of the person, a thirst for interpersonal relationship. The experience of the father, the wealth of the father, is put to death by the son. For the son is the one to knock the father's security out from under him. It is the son's life impulse, his urge toward freedom and the fullness of existence, which demonstrates to the father with unmistakable clarity that everything the son has received from him is marked for death.

The elder son who stays at home continues to accept the goods as goods. He does not expose them to the risk of death, and therefore to the hope of resurrection. He is comfortable in his tranquil unawareness of the father; his deadly lethargy is the real death of the father. The younger son with his negative experiences lays open the goods he has received from the father—wealth, power, value—stripping off their cover to learn that there is danger in them. In fact his love becomes "thingified" and ends up in loneliness; his goods give out, and he is reduced to indigence; the dignity he had from birth is degraded to the point where he is tending pigs. The triumph of life lies in the recognition contained in this epilogue: "I have sinned against heaven and you." It is a recognition in which the father, the one who has given the instruments of life that lead to death, is identified and so also is the son, who lives out the experience of this death.

Fundamentally there is only one human experience, and the rhythm of life is the same for all. The impulse of life has its term in the desert, and from the desert it begins again. There are those who never get to the desert, remaining in an infantile state of human and psychological poverty. It could be said that what plagues our modern technological society is not knowing how to "die." Life is seen as an uninterrupted continuum; our culture pretends to have overcome the law of life, death, and resurrection. It does not know how to accept death and, in fact, denies it.

Artistic representations of the contemporary person show us a burnt-out individual resigned to being always the child, in a kind of infantile beatitude that never unfolds into a full and fecund maturity. While people go like arrows toward the sun and soar among the stars, the being of humanity is enveloped in a deadly quietude. We are cave dwellers with atomic energy in our hands. Perhaps we are like the righteous who bring no joy to heaven because "they have no need to repent," and we are what we are because we protect our life against the demands of every ethical and qualitative evaluation, investing it totally in possession, power, and worth.

One can die by disregarding the instinct of self-preservation, by rejecting existence, and one can die in search of truth, in the great risk of freedom. The death of those who do not "die in the Lord"—in the *Logos*, truth—is beyond redemption. The death of those who die in the Lord is the prelude to resurrection. Resurrection is this identity in which we find ourselves to be children of the Father, reborn. The sign of this identity is the concentration of all our interests in love, in the discovery of the person. "But those things I used to consider gain, I have now reappraised as loss in the light of Christ" (Phil 3,7). The new person is one who has received the "capacity for the other," that is, a genuine capacity to love. We must insist that the capacity to love is human, although we do not receive it as a normal physiological development like ears, eyes, senses. It comes to us after death, it is the capacity of the resurrected. The new person is not the patched-up old person, the old person after a hormone treatment. The new person is the dead one who has risen, the one who was lost and has been found.

The father and the elder son fail to understand each other because they speak two different languages. The son talks about lambs, goats, property, justice and injustice. The father has discovered the person who comes to meet him. The conversation between the father and the elder son is expeditious and a little ironic: "Calm down, don't get upset. You stay in your world. Nobody is going to take it away from you. Let me delight in this new-found joy, the indescribable miracle of dialogue, the novelty of encounter."

The encounter is both epilogue and point of departure because it does not rest on the basis of goods to be shared; it is the journey of two poor people. Through the squandering of the father's goods by the son a new relationship is brought into being. The two of them, in the impoverishment they have experienced, discover a new value, that of touching each other as persons. "What good are goods to me? The one who was dead has come back to life; he who was lost has been found."

I refuse to consider this episode as the "parable of forgiveness": The rake does anything he wants to, and the father finally forgives him. For me it is, in its universal meaning, a parable of love and relationship. The son who left home is not someone forgiven but someone raised from the dead. It is not a question of words but of viewpoint and substance. The forgiveness of sin for the Christian is not the assurance of being washed clean. It is resurrection in which there should be evident a radical change in love and relationship; it is to receive the capacity for the other.

The parable in our day takes on a note that is quite pessimistic. Those who should proclaim the Other, the Savior without whom we cannot be saved, are out of touch with the adventure of faith. Between boredom and contentment, they eat away at our "Christian culture," an inheritance that day by day has less value. They believe, they hope, that they are going to stay until the end at the father's estate, and the fear of losing this security is at the bottom of a pathetic lament which calls for an attitude of respect and silence: "Let me die in the faith I was born in. . . ."

Those who have been stripped of everything have arrived at death by passing through another experience of life: that of love become loneliness, that of possessions transformed into indigence, that of worth into devaluation of the self and of existence. The generation of the fathers is corroded in all its expressions—political, cultural, religious. It is corroded less through protest—which can be checked at its roots, as the father did in *Love Story*—than by the sterility and abandonment in which it is anchored. It is ready to forgive but not to "understand the son," to give all but not to let itself be looked at with a new, young, resurrected gaze. The most evident proof of this is the nonsensical rhetoric with which the fathers send their sons off to die in order to protect the inheritance and the future of the sons. And worse still, and more hypocritically, at the religious level there is talk of reforms, of a breakthrough to new liberties, when meanwhile the sons are being sacrificed in order to save material things.

The human adventure sketched in the parable of the prodigal son is not juvenile foolishness, the daring love affair of adolescents; it is the eternal quest for freedom, the quest of one more human being; it is, fundamentally, a going to the Other, who can free us from loneliness and the sterility of our self. I do not conquer the Other; the Other conquers me. I say this because there can also be a religious alienation and it is more serious than any other. I can take over the symbols with which God approaches me and change them into my property, my power. I can then defend my property to the hilt and still claim it is the property of the Other.

The sign of rebirth is to have broken every static schema in our capacity to see people as they are. "I assure you, I have never found this much faith in Israel. Mark what I say: Many will come from the east and the west and will find a place at the banquet in the kingdom of God with Abraham, Isaac and Jacob" (Mt 8, 10–11). "Father, Lord of heaven and earth, to you I offer praise; for what you have hidden from the learned and the clever you have revealed to the merest children" (Mt 11,25). "I want you to observe that this poor widow contributed more than all the others who donated to the treasury" (Mk 12,43). "This man is a true Israelite. There is no guile in him" (Jn 1,47). To have discovered Christ beyond and more deeply within "Christianity" is manifested in the ability to be poor and accepting, the ability to accept the person, history, the creation. This cannot be achieved by a decision of the will or by a diplomatic ruse; either one delights in people apart from their cultural and worldly framework or one doesn't delight in them. And only those who are reborn, those who have passed through death and have lost all to save their own life—that is, their true identity—can have a liking for the person.

The elder brother cannot accept the one who left home because he is very sure of himself, because he knows perfectly well what good and evil are. Not ever having gone beyond the limits of the law, not being able to imagine another space, another criterion, another way of looking at things, he is in the right. According to the law, Christ is truly guilty, he must die. The law has frozen that man in his superego, into a static mold into which he has earnestly tried to fit his own self.

How alive and contemporary is the parable of the prodigal son in this prophetic hour of the church! Dialogue is often impossible because there is a basic difference of language: *One is the language of the law, the other of prophecy.* People of the law do not tolerate insecurity—what they call imprecision, vagueness. They are not willing to explore the meaning of existence in order to understand that in this existence of sin and error it is still possible for the light of justice and truth to filter in. They have a set of measuring standards; whoever does not meet these standards is liable to condemnation. Those people can bring themselves to accuse and to pardon because they know from their own experience what it costs to adapt oneself to the model, to oblige the real self, with its instincts and demands, to be what it should be; but they cannot understand.

The meaning of life for the elder brother is not a search for light, the journey toward the truth that shines forth in everyone who comes into this world; rather, it consists in being a settled, well-defined, and programmed person. He needs the security of the "anterior, posterior, and exterior"; he would philosophically call it the security of the real, of being itself. Psychologically it is the security of the womb—the fear of leaving the mother's womb, the fear of losing one's life. Prophecy means to look for security in the day-to-day fearlessness of faith. To those who are afraid I would say that the Lord asks of us the kind of faith that martyrs have.

The elder son does not see that the adventure of his brother is motivated by a demand of love, space, history; and even less does he understand that this epilogue in misery and indigence is the point at which all alienations are brought to an end. He is able to discover nothing more than the destruction of a model that was affording his brother security, the breaking up of obedience to an authority which allowed him to live comfortably a life not worked out by himself, not searched for with autonomy. The day he accepted the fact that his brother has shaken the foundation, the order that he fights desperately to save in order to save himself, his reason for existence would end. If he would accept this, he would find himself in the same desert as his brother. And that can't be. The real demon who rules the earth, and it is now easy to identify him, is fear. Tormented by this demon, we now search aggressively and violently for doctrinal and economic security, the security of power, possession, worth. This explains many things in the church, in society, in the family, and in business.

To recognize, as Paul did, that all—those within the law as well as the rebels—arrive at the same desert is the most courageous act that we are capable of. It is the act of birth of the new church that reaches out to the world, becomes truly universal, and is renewed by this fullness. "Appearance does not make a Jew. True circumcision is not a sign in the flesh. He is a real Jew who is one inwardly, and true circumcision is of the heart; its source is the spirit, not the letter. Such a one receives his praise, not from men, but from God" (Rom 2,28–29).

This gentle parable of "forgiveness" shows the dramatic failure of encounter that in time rips apart every human community. It underscores the elder son's envious protest hidden beneath a pretense of objectivity, of good, of truth, of law—of something that is over and above us. But what is really involved is the ability to condemn another, with a tranquil conscience, "apart from his history." *Plato is a friend, but truth is a greater friend* is an adage that has been used to justify the most violent and perverse persecutions. The yoking of the person to a static model allows the hypocritical satisfaction of feeling superior, of judging oneself "different from the others."

The truth—Being—means nothing if it does not liberate the person in truth. The gospel has taught us to discover the *Logos*, the truth, as the light in every person who comes into this world, as the capacity to become truth in the person. And the sign that truth, which is Christ, is within us is our gradual and progressive ability to *"read the event prophetically and receive another prophetically."* I would say, using other words, that it is the ability to see the event and the person in the light of Easter—that is, not statically but in a process of death and resurrection. I never tire of calling attention to the fact that in the parable, while the prodigal son himself is using the language of the law—which is the "language of the home," the idiom he has learned—the father, changed through the pain of the adventure, speaks the language of prophecy. He does not say "Yes, you have sinned and I forgive you" but: "Quick, bring out the finest robe and put it on him; put a ring on his finger and shoes on his feet . . . because he was dead and has come back to life."

The gospel is full of resurrections: not only the resurrection of Lazarus and those of the boy from Naim, of Jairus's daughter, and of Christ but also the resurrections of John, who leaps in his mother's womb, and of the sons of Zebedee, who break away from everyday living and follow Christ. This raising up of the person is a stupendous event—an awakening, an entering into an understanding wholly beyond expectation, a decision for something new, the discovery that he is someone who until that moment was unknown to him. It is a re-creation, the rebirth which Jesus tried to make Nicodemus understand and which reveals itself in the most authentic human journeys: in the little deaths of every day, in the desert where we continually lose ourselves. It takes place in the learned man who comes to Jesus at night, confused in his doctrinal schemata; in the Canaanite woman, beside herself with grief over the sickness of her daughter; in the woman with the flow of blood who, on touching the hem of his garment, feels entering into her the life that had been slipping away from moment to moment; in the centurion, who discovers in the conversation which reminds him of military discipline that there is a power exercising control over his life.

People of faith are those who break out of the cocoon, out of the pattern of their own thought. Truth floods into them and offers them a fresh vision, an entirely new capacity for evaluating people, movements, and things. They are able to see the fire under the ashes, to bring forth life from death. The Christian community, if it is a community of faith, is not one that places intolerable burdens on the shoulders of others, but one that "proclaims the resurrection," one that is capable of seeing, in the ambiguity of life and in the quest where a person is "ruined," a presage of resurrection.

In the parable the father and the son are two reborn people. They embrace at the door of the house and the words the father addresses to his son—devoid at once of severity and of indulgence, words on another wavelength, from another world—lead us into the meaning of prophecy. A relationship that we were accustomed to see in its mathematical rigidity is completely shattered.

No, there are not saviors and saved, those who have salvation and those who need salvation, those who possess truth and those who have wandered off course in the search; there are not teachers and pupils. Only one is the Teacher, the Lord; only one is the truth, the way, the life. Those who do not have the truth, those who have gone in search of it, free the one who stayed home from the temptation of feeling secure, of "thing-ifying" the truth, of idolatry. They reveal to him that God does not "dwell in houses made by men," that he is not within the "wood that burns" but goes to the encounter with his creatures.

The lost son "brings this God home," made *resurrection and re-encounter*, by him, in him, in his adventure. Truly, as Paul says, Christ has torn down the wall of division between the faith and the Gentiles. There are no longer two peoples, but only one. It is the son "dead" and "lost" who announces the resurrection.

6

The Call of the Other

Afterward he went out and saw a tax collector named Levi sitting at his customs post. He said to him, "Follow me." Leaving everything behind, Levi stood up and became his follower.

After that Levi gave a great reception for Jesus in his house, in which he was joined by a large crowd of tax collectors and others at dinner. The Pharisees and the scribes of their party said to his disciples, "Why do you eat and drink with tax collectors and non-observers of the law?"

Jesus said to them,"The healthy do not need a doctor; sick people do. I have not come to invite the self-righteous to a change of heart, but sinners" (Lk 5,27–32).

The one responsible for transmitting the gospel to the "children of the kingdom," engrafting himself in the Hebraic tradition, is not a child of the kingdom but a sinner, a publican, a convert like Zacchaeus. His name is Levi, or Matthew. The sequence of the encounter is very similar to that involving Zacchaeus. There is lacking only the analysis of the interior process, depicted in the decision of Zacchaeus to go out onto the streets of Jericho and climb a tree in order to see the one who would be his guest. Now it is Christ who approaches the office of Levi-Matthew, the tax collector. This man is also searching, judging by the swiftness with which he responds to the invitation to follow the Lord: and Levi, leaving everything behind, stands up and follows him. The gospel stresses the swiftness of the decision.

Whoever has gone through this kind of experience does not know how this moment of "madness" comes about. The psychology of sin and the psychology of the gift of self bear a striking resemblance to each other. We would not sin if we didn't lose our sense of logic, at least for a moment. The decision to sin is freely made; nevertheless, it is completely illogical. One thing we never forget is the yes or the no we have said to God. It is a most illogical moment because the ability to foresee is suspended; it represents an interruption in the continuity of our lives. And yet it is the clearest moment because no happening is more viscerally present to us than the yes or the no. All the episodes that follow are a variation on this moment in which we have decided.

We will never be able to recount our decisions with accuracy, because—at the moment of making them—logic, which is the instrument for doing, is absent. I think this is our difficulty with Confession—that is, the feeling that we are not being truthful when we tell a story that is all too true. Perhaps this is the cause of scrupulosity, which is the morbid fear of not being truthful. God will always recognize us in this acceptance or in this rejection that will loom much larger in our life than all the logical things we could do. The clear and prudent options will never have the bewitching radiance of this "Follow me."

Today we must understand redemption in its sociopolitical dimension; yet we must not lose sight of this liberation from *insecurity*. This illogical and, at the same time, very clear-headed leap that is the response to the "Follow me" represents liberation from insecurity.

The young generation will not be in agreement with that last statement; if I am correct, they will consider me arrogant and out of touch. We are all guests in a rotting palace, members of a bankrupt family, but my generation has known years of prosperity, years of security, has known the time when decision seemed to be an opening of windows to happiness. It was saying yes to stable wealth of ancient origin, sure of the future. My yes, too, is surrounded by darkness, because in all generations love is madness or it is nothing. But in what a climate of security and stability!

My sympathy for the young generation is tinged with remorse. I ask myself what share of the responsibility falls upon each one of us for wasting the inheritance so quickly, letting the ancient house cave in when it seemed so secure for centuries to come—like the walls the Roman republic left us—without searching for another alternative. Our mistake has been to believe in wealth, stability, certainty. In the name of this credulity, we have asked our young people to follow us, giving them as a guarantee, not a personal experience, but objective wealth and stability. But this was not ours to give; it was something apart from ourselves that we had no right to pledge.

Now those who have followed us, fascinated by the power without ever making a commitment to a Person, are leaving us one by one. We ask ourselves if "they had a true vocation," when perhaps we should ask ourselves if we have brought them to the Person who invited them. Or could it be that we have taken them for a walk through the garden or into the picture gallery while in the meantime the walls were crumbling and the termites were gnawing away at the foundations? Do we have the courage to stand in judgment over "those who leave us," we who are the cause of a frustration that perhaps will weigh on them for the rest of their lives? I am tempted to think that even if they had never entered a house in ruins nor gone through vineyards in the process of destruction, they still would probably not have found anything better. To avoid ecclesial structures is not to avoid frustration. But I am aware that the reasoning here is not valid.

The only certainty we can give the young generation is that of Saint Paul: *I know in whom I believe*. . . . Whoever has said yes to Christ—not to a culture, not to an interesting movement, not to a structure but to him—can strengthen the weak and at the same time stimulate a response that will be as faithful in moments of crisis as in moments of clarity.

We must realize that we are not in the year two thousand but in the first year of Christ, that we are not about to enter into a kingdom and enjoy an inheritance already ours but are committed to the building up of the kingdom. We have no guarantee to back us up; there is no insurance to cover the investment of a life. "As they were making their way along, someone said to him, 'I will be your follower wherever you go.' Jesus said to him, 'The foxes have lairs, the birds of the sky have nests but the Son of Man has nowhere to lay his head' " (Lk 9,57–58).

Can the person of this generation, like Levi, answer him with a firm, definitive yes and leave everything to follow him? The present-day sickness is insecurity, which is another name for fear. And it is not a trifling sickness that can be cured without bedrest. It is the cause of war, aggression, and the lack of love. It is the deepest misery. A phrase of Bernanos strikes us as being terribly true today: "Within a short time the modern world will have no spiritual reserves left to do evil with." Our certainty, the clarity with which "Someone" was calling us to do "something," could have provoked an outright rejection, but it demanded a response. We could not pretend to be deaf.

I think that it has been precisely this certainty of having to do something and of having to give something that has betrayed us. We have fallen into idolatry. To define it, there are no better words than these: Idolatry is

to model an object that would be the image of this absolute subject. Man will replace the unbearable presence of the being who is totally free and omnipotent with another presence, product of his ingenuity and his dreams, immediately scaled down because it has come forth from the subjectivity of man himself. . . . Instead of letting himself be modeled in pain by the hand of God, who—and he knows this from experience—will remodel him only by ripping out and destroying what is false in him, man prefers to model God in man's own image. Idolatry is therefore a feverish attempt at *objectivation;* it is the attempt to replace with a created image Him in whose image man is by definition created (D. Barthélemy, *Dieu et son image,* p. 113).

When the chosen people fall into idolatry, God totally destroys human works in order to remake them all over again. I feel that we are in this situation. This definition may leave a way out for those who do not accept the hour of exile, the time of the diaspora in which we find ourselves. And the way out will be to blame idolatry on the "others."

It is obvious that our culture is idolatrous: It leaves no room for transcendence; it tries to fit God somehow into the actions carried out by us and into images that we can manipulate. Secularization and demythologization lend themselves to many errors, in spite of their attempt to give a death-blow to idolatry. As a matter of fact, when they throw idolatry out the door, it manages to get back through the window. The fear of transcendence, of something beyond our control, makes us accept only the image of a god whose movements and intentions we can control. If the true worshipers are not on the alert, keeping their eyes fixed on the invisible, they can unwittingly end up among the idolaters. The idolatrous image has become so diluted in love, solidarity, liberation, poverty, that it has become a mystery, something invisible.

We can defend ourselves from an idol like the golden calf that occupies space, but we can defend ourselves only with great difficulty from this imitation of God that uses the techniques of the spiritual and the invisible. The sacred world and the profane world, which were once distinct, have now become blended in such a way that the frontiers are fuzzy, and we no longer know where we are. We are like the Indians among whom at the moment I am putting my notes together. While they are hunting wild boars or jaguars in the Amazon forest, they do not know at any given moment whether they are in Venezuela, Colombia, or Brazil. This should not upset us; each confusion of frontiers is really a step forward. Frontiers were not created by God but by us. And when they are knocked down, even though it be not by decree but by ignorance, it is always a sign of peace.

It is well to read the Epistle to the Romans as though it were written for us, for our culture. After having dealt with the two cultures, the pagan (profane) and the Israelite (sacred), Paul concludes that both were guilty of idolatry: "Well, then, do we find ourselves in a position of superiority? Not entirely. We have already brought the charge against Jews and Greeks alike that they are under the domination of sin. . . . This means that every mouth is silenced and the whole world stands convicted before God" (Rom 3, 9–19). Idolatry is present not only in the "profane" world but also in the "sacred" world. We have tried to define the essence of this Presence with a precise cultural model, limiting its action to a circle controlled by ourselves. The loving and intense effort of the saints to "see God" is not curiosity but a plunge into the ocean of being in order to be real, an entering into the essence of God in order to be molded; but it easily becomes in our eyes a form of idolatry. Just as we put in a glass case the clothing the saints wore during their earthly pilgrimage and attribute to it a certain miraculous power, something divine that clings to it, so the journals of their search become the search itself, and their experience of God becomes our God.

We feel that we are exempt from searching for someone already found and from repeating a dangerous journey of exploration, now that the land has been explored. Thus our relationship with the Other becomes an acceptance of an itinerary that is not ours, in admiration of an experience another has had in our stead. We have become more accustomed to trembling with fear, weeping for joy or sadness, through reading a book than through actually venturing forth to this strange "lunar" world, and the experience of God is necessarily experience of the world because we find God in a tangible way in the goodness that envelops all the happenings of the world. We see God reflected "in the lilies of the field, the grass which blooms today and is thrown on the fire tomorrow." We see God as beauty; we discover God in things that happen, as the goodness that gives meaning to everything.

Those who—like Saint Augustine, Saint Bonaventure, or Saint Thomas—have searched for God have seen him in their world; they have seen him in the wild flowers that blossomed under their feet and afterwards were burned; they have seen him in the happenings in which they were involved and in those by which they were swept along. I prefer to see them as searchers for the image of God rather than heresy fighters. We will not come to know God as long as we live in an absurd world. We can accept and live with mystery but not with the absurd. Mystery molds and forms us; the absurd destroys us. Mystery makes us break into tears; the absurd brings us to suicide. That world in which the saints looked for the footprints of Christ and the direction of the Exodus no longer exists. In their writings we cannot look for anything other than witness, a fidelity to God, the testimony to the fact that man can search for security through risk. We are left with the clothing of the saints; they themselves have eluded us. Here is our idolatry. For security we have adopted the writings about a search experience. The itinerary of the saints was only a method, and we have taken it to be the content of the search, making it our principal resource. We are like the heirs of a rich man who take his goods but reject the sweat, labor, astuteness, the road to the accumulation of wealth. Thus the image of God and of the world that we get from the saints we have made idols of is not the true image of the Creator.

The church today is found to be *poor*, but we all try to minimize this discovery, to pulverize it in order that the system can digest it, so to speak. The church is poor, and this rock fallen from heaven into the pool of a somnolent Christianity has stirred the water a bit. An initiative has gotten under way to decipher and reveal the meaning of this discovery. We resort to every kind of jargon to define the emptiness, the nothing, the nonexistent. All our efforts to define poverty indicate once more to what degree we are sick from idolatry. We are so accustomed to the little statues we make by hand that we now feel obliged to make an image of the most recently canonized saint: Our Lady of Poverty. But the poverty of which the Holy Spirit speaks and which brought about the most important intuition of the Vatican Council is for us merely a notice, an announcement of the next visit from God. "Now, I will let you know what I mean to do to my vineyard: Take away its hedge, give it to the grazing, break through its wall, let it be trampled! Yes, I will make it a ruin; it shall not be pruned or hoed, but overgrown with thorns and briers; I will command the clouds not to send rain upon it. The vineyard of the Lord of hosts is the house of Israel, and the men of Judah are his cherished plant. He looked for judgment, but see, bloodshed: for justice, but hark, the outcry!'' (Is 5, 5–7). If we could see the gentleness there is in these words, we would stop being afraid. These are sad words but not frightening. Nevertheless, to accept them as words of love, it is necessary to know Him who pronounces them. Having lost sight of Him, we find these words unbearable. They are too much for us and we disregard them. The idol is the product of fear of God.

Poverty is an idol whenever it is a parallel poverty, looked upon apart from and counter to that message. It is an idol whenever we lack the courage to look upon the countenance of God who comes to us with the plan of impoverishing us, stripping us bare, destroying our security so that we will find ourselves alone and naked before him. Hope awaits us beyond despair, at the moment our easy optimism—which is not hope—has been burnt away. God destroys, but he leaves signs for us to recognize the kingdom. He does not leave ''stone upon stone,'' but he does leave the foundations, so that we will always be able to find the center of the kingdom. One sign is that all messages unfailingly arrive there. The church, for those who wish to understand this, has announced the design of the future world, has understood its own place, after the exile, after the diaspora. For those who can see, there are signs of love in rage.

Poverty is not a virtue: we do not make ourselves poor. Even in the case of chosen poverty, that poverty is realized by aligning oneself with those whom violence has made poor. Being poor means being stripped of every guarantee of security. And poverty becomes a beatitude when, after having felt the shudder of emptiness, of death, after the emptiness has destroyed in us the last root of self-interest, we discover that it is precisely this absolute insecurity that leads to the deepest kind of security. There is no other way to escape insecurity and the radical incapacity to make true options—a consequence of insecurity—than to let all kinds of security be ripped from our hands. All these kinds of security are the idols which we cannot serve and at the same time serve the living God as well. We must let them be ripped from our hands, not throw them away spontaneously, because this would be a gesture of defense and fear.

I would ask all Christian "poverty fanatics" to give up this search. Non-being, the nonexistent, is nowhere to be found. In the authentic plan of religious life, poverty ought to be a training ground, a challenge to hope; whereas in fact, little by little, we have been transforming it into a thing, an idol. Now the church, which is the unifying center of the whole of God's message and the broadcast center of the permanent dialogue of God with us, has received notice that it will be poor, that it will be "made poor." This is the first stage of the intervention of God, who is Being, and God does not wish to destroy unless it be to build up.

But it is normal and just that the destruction should have the appearance of destruction and that hope should arrive just as it is fading, leaving only the root buried, invisible, which because of its hidden condition is of no use to us. We see, through the terror diffused within the walls of the kingdom and through the desperate attempts to save at least something, that the destruction is real, that the discipline of God is not a comedy. All the seminars on poverty, psychoanalyzed, are nothing more than the fear of God, the fear of losing, the terror of being "stripped." They are exactly the opposite of what is announced on the program. Bernanos says that the highest form of hope is despair overcome, not despair pushed aside, which is something else. We have no power of decision over poverty; we cannot decide the degree, the shape, or the hour. The important thing in the hour of poverty is not to bargain.

Abraham could have negotiated or decided his service of God—"allow yourself to serve and you'll make out well." He could have given up his cattle, his house; he could have done without Sarah, now that she had given him a man-child. He could have burned everything. But this would not have been poverty, because the emptiness decided on by us is always full; that we should decide to give up something is always an acquisition. The more we talk about poverty, the more we are contaminated with property. We can only prepare ourselves to let God impoverish us.

We have a situation today that is similar to the situation that held sway when Jesus appeared in the world. When Jesus criticizes the Pharisees, they answer him: "We are descendants of Abraham. . . . Never have we been slaves to anyone. What do you mean by saying, 'You will be free'?" (Jn 8,32). What always annoys us is this "you will be"; we want it now, not later. We cannot receive truth because we have security in our hands and do not want to let go of it. Perhaps what God is asking of the church today is that it abandon the doctrinal security with which it has judged the world. If the decision were to be in our hands, it would be impossible. How do you distinguish fidelity to the Word from the passion to rule? How do you free the real message from the cultural context? Security certainly comes to the church out of an authentic experience, out of an encounter with God; but time, emptying out this experience, has transformed it into an archaeological relic. In Christ's time the words: "We are the descendants of Abraham, disciples of Moses" had the same meaning as the words we hear today: "We are Thomists, or we have Saint Augustine for a father." If the church were not undergoing a continuous transformation, re-creation, rejuvenation, the profound changes that are taking place within it would be incomprehensible. The history of the kingdom is the history of a living organism, of a true relationship which, like all relationships, has its negative and tormenting aspects. The only thing we know is that the relationship is kept alive tenaciously and obstinately on one side, and that for this reason it will never be broken off. The indefectibility of the kingdom hinges totally on the fidelity of God, and it is taken care of out of our sight, invisibly. When we try to relate it to historical visibility, making predictions on this hypothesis, we are imitating the gypsies reading their fortune in the cards.

We have entered into the historical space of defeat, destruction. The agony of the church, which is the center of the world, is proof that the whole world and our whole culture is in agony. A sign of this is the lucidity with which the church continues to send forth its messages and the utter impossibility of using them as an instrument to restructure our culture.

The tragic disproportion between the church that says that it teaches and the church that acts is not due only to natural human cowardice but to the fact that a culture and a world must die and the world that is being born is not yet clear. There are blossoms here and there, but they are hidden beneath the wintry mantle that covers the earth. And no one, not even the church, can see them. The church must live with the inability to confront the present culture. To me it is stupendous to be present for and live through this paradoxical spectacle: The church holds onto its security, its strength and vitality, and at the same time is part of this insecurity, this death of a world and a culture. It is difficult for people in the church to accept death, and we, like everyone else, run around looking for security because we do not have the Lord. We do not know how to die in the Lord—an easy thing to preach and sing about but difficult to put into practice. Nobody can give us a guarantee of security because we live under the decision that we are not part of, to destroy all forms of security. This is precisely why the margin of security the church had gained in the areas of power, politics, and doctrine has crumbled, and within a short time the church will be without land and without security of any kind, becoming increasingly poor.

A phrase of the pope's, embedded in an address given to the nobility, acquires a prophetic note: "The church is poor, it has nothing to give." Perhaps at that moment the pope, like the prophets, did not see the abyss of poverty into which the church would tumble within a very short time. It would be poor because all the certainties, all the visible documents proving God is with it, would be snatched from its hands. Through this crisis I am sure that a great change will take place: The church will again defend the documents, the proofs that God is with the church, that God *has his kingdom in history, instead of using the documents for its own defense.* The difference here is substantial: We understand it clearly on the human, individual level, even when it is not easy to mark neatly the boundaries of the two fields. There are certainly those who make of the Word of God and of anything that is "religious" a shield of defense, and there are certainly those who "lose" their own life, in sacrifice, to defend and witness to the Word of God and everything that is of God.

The inauguration of a new era for the kingdom is announced by the Council when it affirms that the era of the "monarchy" is over and that the era of the "prophets" has begun, an era of hope and certainty amid the smoking ruins and the total destruction. Must we go back to the catacombs? No, this privilege is not given to us. The catacombs are from the era of force, the epoch of the "king." Insecure people can drop the atomic bomb on the world, but they cannot make martyrs. They will kill the prophet who threatens their little provisional security, the refuge for the moment from the alarm, but they cannot produce an epoch of martyrs. Martyrdom is born of a confrontation of ideas; it supposes a love of truth, a certainty, which is precisely what is lacking in our culture. We have faith only in movement, in progress. But becoming is an endless search, a truth that continuously moves further away and that does not even allow itself to be found. Christians, although they may not be able to adapt themselves to the world, should adapt themselves to the time of crisis, to their lack of definition, to their insecurity, to their anguish. They should accept existentially the present and real relationship that God has decided to have with his espoused People.

There are indeed analogies between those who model themselves exclusively upon our culture and those who are called to serve the Presence, to make up the small remnant, and this is because both groups seem to share the same insecurity. Nevertheless there is a profound difference. It is the "poor" security of Abraham, Moses, and the prophets, renewed by Christ. We should not count on the triumphs of the past, the treasures hoarded up, what we possess, "because all will be burned like straw" (Mt 23, 38). We should count on the Person: "Come after me and I will make you fishers of men" (Mt 4, 19). We should count on him as Abraham did, who believed that from sterility and death would come forth life.

We all share the insecurity of our culture. It is not intellectual weakness or an incapacity for logic; it is the lack of love that has made us poor. First love is betrayed; and after that, truth. It is certain that the world is in trouble because it is incapable of truth, but this is due to its incapacity for love. The world goes on living because it has in its hands the chain of hypotheses that allows it to go from one link to the other; but its life is provisional. Life is not life when we lack the kind of security that permits us to look one another in the face and to continue to live together without destroying ourselves. There is no future for human life, at least in the epoch we are now in, unless we manage to cure ourselves of this insecurity that makes us aggressive, violent, incapable of sitting down beside one another. And no doctrine or truth can cure this insecurity. The church says: "I am the truth that can save the world," but what good is a truth that people cannot understand? It is like the Eucharist that loses its value when it does not bring about community or unite people. Unity and love are the signs of the presence and the operative power of the Word and of the sacrament. If it is incapable of uniting us, of moving us toward genuine communication and curing the insecurity that threatens us from within and prevents us from seeing people and things as our "brothers and sisters," this means that it has lost its power. Jesus spoke of the salt that loses its capacity to flavor and of the yeast that does not raise the dough.

Those who defend the system of truth, believing that they are defending God, identifying it with the experience of God and with the signs of his presence among us, ought to stop and think for a moment. Think—instead of continuing to repeat, like a dismal refrain, that our culture is empty of God, that it is going to ruin, that it will never give us any security, that there is no hope for us. Why do they not have the courage to admit *as a consequence* that the world has no salt or yeast and that the doctrine of their system cannot save because it is a remedy grown too old? I remember the words of Bernanos: "When they dream about rekindling the bonfires, they do it not so much with the notion of hurling the wicked into them as with the hope of heating up their own lukewarmness, which the Lord vomits out of his mouth." What prevents us from getting around the problem is the habit of looking at the world from our angle and hoping that sinners will come to us (that is, the opposite of what Christ preaches). This is the case even when physically it would seem that we are ones who are reaching out to the "sinners." Yet it would seem to be so simple a thing, and above all so full of results. The present culture is disoriented because the compass is broken. The ship is off course, not because of mechanical defects but because it lacks "direction." We have not been faithful to the controls of the gospel.

The presence of Christ is recognized by the union it effects and the community it creates. The efficaciousness of truth is recognized in the unity it produces, in the concrete decision it elicits, and therefore in its capacity to be understood. A philosophy and a theology might have once been the dwelling-place of God; but they can cease to be, and then the sign of this Presence is idolatrous. During the journey through the desert, the bronze serpent, on being raised up on a pole, communicated life. . . . "Whenever anyone who had been bitten by a serpent looked at the bronze serpent, he recovered" (Num 21, 9). And it was not the serpent who gave life: "For he who turned toward it was saved, not by what he saw, but by you, the savior of all" (Wis 16, 7). Later, King Hezekiah, who "pleased the Lord, just as his forefather David had done, . . . destroyed the bronze serpent . . . that Moses had made, because up to that time the Israelites were burning incense to it" (2 Kgs 18, 3–4). In faithfulness to God, the king destroyed what had been in another time a sign of the Presence and what little by little had been turning into an idol. We have an incurable tendency to fall into idolatry.

We should have the courage to acknowledge that if human culture—which is a means of relationship and communion—has become a vehicle of division and confusion, if it lacks a principle of unification, it is because it has no salt, it is dough without yeast. The small margin of defense of the "idolaters" is possible only in a dualist division: our culture and the world's culture. But this division is no longer acceptable since the clarifications of the Vatican Council: From now on there is but one culture, one human search. Either there is a culture of communion or one of division; but there will never be a culture of total communion, it will always be ambiguous. At any rate, whether there will be greater or less communion depends on whether there is more or less salt and on the degree of efficacy of the yeast. In the measure in which the old idolatrous structures fall, a Christian culture identified with truth will abandon the religious structures reinforced by economic laws and secularized to the hilt; and we will have, present and strong, the "small remnant." Those who have no intention of abandoning Christ will have to accustom themselves to living as a small remnant, that is, in a space and time that is prophetic. We are looking for false reconciliations, "to tear a piece from a new coat to patch an old one" (Lk 5, 36).

Today, I feel the presence in history of the prophet Jeremiah's gesture: "Thus said the Lord: Go, buy a potter's earthen flask. . . . Go out toward the valley of Ben-hinnom, at the entrance of the Potsherd Gate; there proclaim the words which I will speak to you. . . . And you shall break the flask in the sight of the men who went with you and say to them: Thus says the Lord of hosts: Thus will I smash this people and this city as one smashes a clay pot so that it cannot be repaired" (Jer 19,1–11). I avail myself here of the commentary of Barthélemy:

What does this condemnation mean? It means that in the eyes of God, the existence of Judah as a kingdom, the existence of the temple, are things that had to be destroyed. It is high time that from this people or, better still, from the ruins of this people, should be born finally the remnant, the seed that would give birth to another people. This false security in the political realm (kingdom) and in the religious realm (temple) has to be torn away from Israel so that it will understand that the important thing is not to preserve the existing provisional structure but to experience the pangs of the birth that would reach toward the reality of the "last times" that God is making ready. God wishes to see the political and religious structures destroyed, like a mason who takes away the timbering that does nothing more than clutter up the finished building (*Dieu et son image*, p. 202).

The priest Pashur does not understand that all these gestures that make a pretense of being directed to the Lord are nothing more than a perpetual compensation for another justice that is lacking. To reject the prophetic time and to continue living in

another time, anachronistically, is not only to condemn the
self to personal insecurity but also to retard the formation of
the "remnant of Israel," that is, not to work for the coming of
God's kingdom.

History repeats itself: we have the prophetic attitude and the
priestly attitude. In good times the two lines meet and com-
plement each other. As long as the priestly function is faithful
and the sign is not wasted, we have integration. When the
worship of God is emptied of its content and becomes mere
ritual and an instrument for glorifying human beings or in-
stitutions, under the pretext of glorifying God, prophecy is
born of the rupture. The sign of the "new times" is the renewal
of worship that comes about through a crisis, through a moment of darkness, of emptiness: "Believe me, woman, an hour
is coming when you will worship the Father neither on this
mountain nor in Jerusalem" (Jn 4, 21). The sign will be persecution: "The Son of Man must first endure many sufferings, be
rejected . . . " (Lk 9, 22).

What should a disciple of Christ be like in the prophetic
time? It is difficult to say because the spirit is free, and I believe
that God breathes on whom he will. Originating with God,
new creations come about; but we cannot renounce life. And
life means essentially *judging, adoring, loving.* If any of these
three functions is lacking in us, our life is incomplete, we are
vegetables, our life is not full. In the time of exile, in the harsh
epoch of purification, we cannot renounce our existence. Nor
can we hope, because tomorrow does not belong to us. God
can ask our life of us but not total destruction. On the contrary,
the darkest moments are the moments of God; they are the
moments that are especially filled with his presence. Those
who have been talking about the death of God have been
saying, without understanding it, something quite true. God
does not die; what dies is the visible structure of his kingdom,
the sign of the Presence, which now becomes more obscure,
more mysterious, but perhaps more within us. "He prunes
away every barren branch, but the fruitful ones he trims clean
to increase their yield" (Jn 15, 2).

Apologetics is replaced by prophetic preaching, which seeks

out the sign of this Presence in God's world, in human creations, in what is "outside"—but that does not mean accepting
everything through a kind of syncretism. When apologists
have in their hands the synthesis of truth, they adore a culture,
a sign, an expression in which the Presence has revealed itself,
and they hold onto it as their dearest treasure. They see the
prophetic search as treason to the truth. They see two opposed
cultures: the one totally of the truth, the other totally in error,
whereas the prophetic eye looks for the sign of this Presence in
all the ambiguous expressions of the human search. In the
center of the kingdom this function exists; *Gaudium et Spes* and
certain other papal encyclicals are hesitant prophetic glances at
the world. They are hesitant because they do not accept our
epoch bravely as an epoch of destruction, of defeat, and therefore of hope. They look kindly and indulgently on the field of
the "neighbor," but they go on seeing their own field as
model. The centers of prophecy will point out the indestructible foundations on which the kingdom, little by little, will be
rebuilt.

Destroying structures, driving us into exile, God will yet not
abandon us but will purify us, restoring to us a direct relationship without the need of signs that have become empty of his
Presence. The search for this Presence must be made patiently
and painfully, not any longer within structures but in the
diaspora. "They will come from the east and the west." God
looks for true worshipers wherever and however he wishes.
To find him, we must look exclusively for him, wanting nothing else. We must slough off a materialistic and smothering
security. The sign of the Presence is no longer to be found in the
glory of an apparent kingdom but in people of the diaspora, in
a world that in no way has the countenance of the kingdom.

In this prophetic epoch, everyone lacks the means of helping the other to dispel insecurity. In the correspondence that
has arrived for me here in the wilderness I found a long letter
from a young male religious very close to me. I quote a little of
what he had to say: "Against whom and against what is this
anguish? I see myself as in a mirror. And I see myself as so
weak, so poor, so divided, that I ask myself if it is worthwhile

to go on insisting. Only a short while ago when I drank from the chalice at mass, I was seized with a terrible urge to throw it against the wall and break it. And it wasn't even a revolt of faith. If at least it were that! It was something else. A kind of deaf and silent storm that came to the surface after raging underneath for years, in some hidden little corner of my topography which I neither know nor control. It is this wandering around the borders of being-a-person, of the being-in of faith, of the being-in of history, without managing it, either through impotence or cowardice, that again has me on the ropes."

The young generation is certainly having to contend with a psychological insecurity that comes from a "loveless economic family." And there is a cultural insecurity that is the fruit of the industrial and economic culture, designed to create, produce, occupy space, forgetting that our primary task is the interpersonal relationship, something that we are becoming increasingly incapable of. I don't know which comes first: is psychological insecurity the fruit of cultural insecurity, or vice versa? At any rate, there is no point in establishing a priority.

There is no reason to offer this young man an arrogant, offensive, hypocritical security, bragging about my nest egg in the bank that can see the two of us through. And this is precisely what the men of the church have done for centuries, exposing their patrimony to be slowly and inexorably consumed by the advancing culture.

Nevertheless there is a security not founded on what we have in our hands or what we have inherited, a security that comes to us from a Person who is "before us." Christ had nothing to offer: today we are once again at the point of departure and we go forth from the shores of Capernaum toward the world and a history unknown to us. We cannot offer security, and yet we can give another "security" more solid because it is incarnate, existential. I would say that we are going from the regime of inheritance to the regime of friendship. The young generation can understand only a faith that is expressed in valiant decisions. The experience of faith that I live will be so authentic as to enable me to be tossed into emptiness only if I know how to read my time, present and future, without hesitating, without accepting false support, without trying to recapture in some way the triumph that was never mine. A discourse given to the people of the Old Testament and found in Deuteronomy can illustrate this: "It is not your children, who have not known it from experience, but you yourselves who must now understand the discipline of the Lord your God; his majesty, his strong hand and outstretched arm . . . " (Dt 11, 2). The Bible transmits to us the experience that different generations have had of God. When it communicates to those who accept it as a souvenir, with a feeling of sufficiency and superiority, God himself destroys this security. We of another generation can only transmit a security that is neither visible nor tangible: "Our eyes have seen." "You can trust Him and throw yourself into the emptiness." But this experience cannot be transmitted with words; it can only be communicated with life. The prophetic time is the time of the kingdom in ruins and the time of the new creation.

This does not mean that we have to put up with mental confusion and disorder but that we should become used to seeing truth begin to sprout where we least expect it, to see new creations appear on ground we thought sterile. And this literally means that we really accept not knowing where we will be able to lay our head. Tomorrow Christians will be few in number and "religious" even less. This very distinction is outdated, but I use it as a shortcut. Only the courage of Christians can revive a culture that is terribly strong and terribly insecure, and that needs only the breath of hope.

Therefore when a young man asks me if in our world of insecurity he can commit himself like Matthew, who leaves all to follow Jesus, I answer: "If you have heard His voice, the voice of the Other, you can hurl yourself head first and the more vertical your fall, the more surely you will be saved." I like the supreme indifference of Christ, who let the rich young man go away without bargaining with him, refusing to give him any kind of guarantee. After the discourse in the synagogue at Capernaum, he declares that he is willing to let everyone go away and to start all over from the beginning. He doesn't try to hold on to the elect with swimming pools, basketballs, or tennis courts. "Follow me!" he says. This is where we are today, not willingly but because this is the present stage of the kingdom's history.

Luke's description in chapter five is remarkable. Levi puts on a banquet for friends. He has two things in mind—to say farewell to his office and to let his friends know that he has received grace. It is no small thing to have been freed from the terrible loneliness of money, of concern over self—and therefore the nausea of uselessness—and to have committed oneself to the kingdom. I don't know if Levi understood all this at once. It is something we discover little by little, searching constantly and exclusively for this Presence, not looking back at the things left behind, centering everything on this experience. It is worthwhile to leave everything to find the self, to get out from under the state of discouragement, of alienation—of being and yet not being—that my friend speaks of. Modern culture, existentialist, Marxist, structuralist, the drug culture, is for me the clearest possible commentary on the words of Jesus: "What is it worth to a man to gain the whole world if he loses his life?" Of what value is it to us to possess the world and to conquer space if we are alienated? Indeed to find oneself again is well worth a banquet. "He was joined by a large crowd of tax collectors and others at dinner." The guests are not pious persons; they belong to Levi's circle, to his clan. And this scandalizes. Jesus answers the criticism leveled at him by the world of the true believers—who have banquets only "among ourselves"—with a touch of irony: "I have come not to invite the self-righteous to a change of heart, but sinners." Not to invite those who feel "sure" of themselves but those who feel "unsure."

His radical approach does not lead us to think that sinners alone have a right to his visit, but only that the just, if they are to become part of his circle, must see themselves as "sinners," i.e., as poor and insecure. Another young man wrote to me: "When I was a child I wanted to find a man who was wise, secure, at peace; I thought he would give me security. Now I

realize that I am alone and that I must find security for myself."
I felt that in writing to me he was cutting me off and really
saying to me: "Please get it out of your head that you have to
counsel me." At first glance, it seemed that my response ought
to have been: "Why then are you writing to me, wasting your
time and mine? If you're not asking anything from me, why do
you write? It would seem to be a web of contradictions. 'I am
looking for you, and I don't want you; I need you, but you
have nothing to give me. I am writing to you and I expect a
quick answer but, please, no advice!' " This contradiction
which characterizes the dialogue between the generations
seems to me clear and fair. "Don't give me anything of yours; I
only want to know that you exist, that *you are still around, still
hanging in there.* Because if you're still around, it's because you
have a reason for living." This is all we can give the young,
from close up or from far away. The old man does not dish out
wisdom as in the past because —so it is said today— there is no
wisdom. Well, he could still give hope. Those who still claim to
impart wisdom feel frustrated because "wisdom" today, being
responsible for structures that are indestructible, inhuman,
and insecure, has been discredited.

The church today is not prepared in the cultural and pastoral
field to dialogue with "sinners." Nevertheless the church
could transform this poverty into triumph. It lacks any kind of
preparation for dialogue with the various cultures, but it can
give people the only thing they really need: hope. How can it
be understood that the culture, at the very time that it is
tragically insecure, has no need of us Christians? This can only
be understood when the church is accepted by the young and
the poor—when we have finally gotten rid of the notion of
"wanting to convert them," of wanting "to do good for them."

I have come to realize this while being among the Makiritar
Indians, who have held together as an ethnic group and have
kept their own culture, defending themselves with *pride and
self-sufficiency.* They had no other arms to defend themselves
from us, from our culture. Have they at times thought that the
young have no other arms than these to defend themselves?
They are as insecure as other people; they have the same

psychic fragility found in the children of the directors of General Motors. Would they ask for my help if they were not afraid that I would try to foist my culture onto them? Can I offer them a security that would not be "capitalist," crystallized, objective, *made in Europe* or *made in the USA*? Could I infuse a hope that arises from humility, in the slough of despond of a culture? This is the question that is put to adults, to the church, to those who up till now have believed themselves to have the right to teach. The dialogue with the cultures and with atheists cannot come about if we adopt a stance of "respect," of "tolerance," of "pity." It can only come about if those who have given for centuries now have nothing to give and see themselves as poor. Christianity will not be "poor" until God despoils it through the painful process he periodically uses with his people.

This morning I was reading a page from Isaiah that is at once moving and funny. It has to do with the episode about the sickness of King Hezekiah, in which all kinds of human behavior are at play: fear, ambition, avarice, and faith. Hezekiah seems to be a pilgrim who goes to the sanctuary to be cured of a cancer: "Thus says the Lord: 'Put your house in order, for you are about to die; you shall not recover.' Then Hezekiah turned his face to the wall and prayed to the Lord: 'O Lord, remember how faithfully and wholeheartedly I conducted myself in your presence, doing what was pleasing to you.' And Hezekiah wept bitterly." Then the Lord, because of his tears, gave him another fifteen years of life and liberated him from the invader. Later Hezekiah sings for joy and expresses a thought that is typically biblical and which sums up the meaning of our relationship with God: I give you thanks because you let me live; if I were dead, how could I sing of your strength and goodness? "For it is not the nether world that gives you thanks, nor death that praises you; neither do those who go down into the pit await your kindness. The living, the living give you thanks, as I do today. Fathers declare to their sons, O God, your faithfulness" (Is 38). This man who loves life, who pleads with tears that he may not die, finds the "theological argument" to convince God: I am not in the world to *do* or to *give*, but to *witness.* And the fact that I live is proof that one can hope and trust.

Reading the details of Levi's conversion attentively, I sense that there are riches in it that we have not yet discovered, perhaps because we have yet to live through the situations that would create in us the need for these words. If some exegete should tell me that this passage belongs somewhere else, it would not matter to me. Let me read it here. The pharisaical world is unable to understand the Prophet's eating with sinners, and Christ defends himself with the usual argument: Are people worth more than the Sabbath? Then his adversaries have recourse to the strong argument about fasting. A saint, a prophet, is one who fasts, who doesn't attend banquets of this kind. And his answer strikes me as most profound: "Can you make guests of the groom fast while the groom is still with them?" His answer is not on the same wavelength; he has turned the argument completely around. He could have replied that fasting is not observed all through the year, that there are exceptions. It would not have been difficult to find answers in moralistic terms, but the answer he gives takes us away from this approach. You have the law; my followers have the bridegroom, the friend. You see your fidelity to the law as essential and sacrosanct: they see fidelity to the friend. We are talking two different languages, we are on two different planes. But this is not dialogue. "No one tears a piece from a new coat to patch an old one." It is a strong answer given with disdain. A new kind of relationship comes into being, one no longer resting on fidelity to the law but calling for fidelity to the person. The hope that brings security is not materialized —"thingified"—in a culture but remains a thread, tenuous but strong, uniting one person with another. It is a relationship with the Transcendent that finds its human expression in friendship—a friendship secured on one side, intangibly, by absolute fidelity. One side can betray, vacillate, go under; the other can not.

It would seem as if this vision threatened to transform Christianity—essentially ecclesial, that is to say, communitarian—into an individualist and irrational relationship. It is an attempt that crops up continually in the history of Christianity. Yet this is not so. The bond of union in the church, in this hour of diaspora, is no longer tradition, the past, but the promise, the hope. It is not so much the kingdom of the past but the kingdom to come. The past, for the Twelve who were commissioned to build the kingdom, is not empty; on the contrary it is full of history, traditions, laws, personages. What meaning does this have for them? What should they build and what should they destroy? The past is the history of an obstinately faithful God who does not abandon his people and who is inexplicably faithful to his promise. This stubborn friendship of God—which those who experience transmit from one generation to the next—is manifested in military setbacks, in the tyrannies that push the people into idolatry, in the loyal-to-God monarchies, in the hour of liturgical splendor and in the hour of darkness, of slavery, of destruction. The eyes of those who have seen transmit it to those who live in darkness. The past endorses hope inasmuch as it is the bearer of a person and of a friendship. It has value and, at the same time, it does not. It has value as a foundation for hope whereas it has been "emptied" of content by the new. This explains the apparent contradiction in the violent dialogue between Christ and the Pharisees. Granted that in the first part the accent is placed on newness, the new, one could come to believe that people prefer new wine in new bottles. Nevertheless, this exchange closes on a note that, at first sight, is disconcerting: "No one, after drinking old wine, wants new. He says, 'I find the old wine better' " (Lk 5,39). All the past, the old, is repudiated as thing, law, tradition, culture, history, because time and people change continuously. But it is not repudiated as the history of a friendship that endures, of a fidelity that is never destroyed, without which hope is not hope because it has no roots, undergoes no trials, has no life.

We no longer have many "ecclesiastical vocations" in the sense of affiliating oneself with a ministry, signing up for an activity, enrolling in a clan. But we will always have the calls of Christ: "Follow me." And it will come wherever, however, and to whomever he wishes: "Follow me," to continue building up the kingdom, invisible yet unfailing. You can turn back, not to see the dead and bury the dead, but only to rediscover the invisible yet certain, concrete, and incarnate hope in the life of a person and of a number of people. This *poor* certainty is the only thing those of my generation can offer to the generation coming along.

7

Clear Eyes

On their journey Jesus entered a village where a woman named Martha welcomed him to her home. She had a sister named Mary who seated herself at the Lord's feet and listened to her words. Martha, who was busy with all the details of hospitality, came to him and said, "Lord are you not concerned that my sister has left me to do the household tasks all alone? Tell her to help me."

Then the Lord in rèply said to her: "Martha, Martha, you are anxious and upset about many things; one thing only is required. Mary has chosen the better portion and she shall not be deprived of it" (Lk 10, 38–42).

Let us not ask for an identification card from the two sisters who offer hospitality to the Friend. Does it matter? They are two women, and it is very probable that Mary is the "sinner." Certainly she has had a long and painful experience of love. There is no doubt but that she is a person who has come out of the shell of her own self.

The choice of Jesus has given rise to different interpretations, to polemical and exaggerated antitheses between the active and contemplative life, and it has also given rise to the search for a "contemplative state," often identified with a flight from the world and therefore from life. The hyperactive proselytes of the kingdom defend Martha by canonizing her, since they cannot tolerate the quiet, dreamy person, settled in an amorous inertia that does not change the world. I think our slowness in attempting to decipher the meaning of this encounter is justified, since the event touches a vital side of the "human," alive in us. *What is the better portion that Mary has chosen?* To remain seated at the feet of the Master, listening to him? Seen from the outside, the situation leads us to the immediate conclusion that there is a fecund and useful inertia and a useless kind of activity, that idleness can be more truly human than activity. Thus, looking at the literal sense of the words, we see that idleness is definitely human, activity merely provisionally so.

It is pointless to demonstrate that there is a useless kind of activity, since this is a theme discovered by our culture. Our economic culture, extraordinarily active and efficient, has to its credit an enormous balance of wars, divisions, and—above all—that which seems to be its specific trait, of insecurity and fear of tomorrow. It has separated time from space, and while it conquers space, it is pursued by time. Do we not have here the root cause of the imbalance between technical progress and "human" progress? Many very active lives result at the end in a person embittered, destroyed, with no way out. The young generation sees the limitations and the final chapter of an epoch centered on productive and creative effort under the label of the "economic." Is it only because of love of the *dolce vita* that the young refuse to work, or drop out of college? It is important for now that a light shadow of doubt has been cast over the value of activity. We have always viewed "idleness" as the "father of vices" because of the grim light projected upon it by the popular proverb. But activity is the mother of wars of injustice, of oppression, of the evil that reigns in the world.

Nevertheless I don't think that this episode, so fresh and human, that the artist-doctor Luke narrates establishes an antithesis between idleness and activity. The conclusion goes much deeper: Mary has discovered the absolutely Other, the Other absolutely irreducible to the self. And this discovery is at the root of her profound wholeness, *of her true love for others,* of her integrity. It is not that Martha is absorbed in household chores—that is purely coincidental. The Master's observation is not brought on by the collection of plates and casseroles but by the fact that Martha has not yet found the other; she has not gone down into the depths. To be involved in many things constitutes her existential situation. Her self is still exteriorized; it is looking to others for security, joy, shelter. And therefore necessarily, even though she does not want to, she uses, instrumentalizes, thingifies; she does not accept. Mary receives and is received. Martha clings, whether she dominates or is submissive, even though she does not know it, at least consciously. Therefore her relationships are neither liberated nor liberating. She projects onto others the plurality that is within her and concerns herself; and thus the other does not feel accepted, loved, understood, seen for what he is: a unity, a self that is one and unique. Instead, he is viewed through the prism of a multiplicity of things. She does not accept the Other who presents himself to the self and commits it to a constant and essential "oppositeness."

The self thrusts outward in search of security, of objects and persons. The search is provisional; our encounter with others has a disrupting effect that is the preparation for a decentering of the self—for self-denial. It is like a prelude to the acceptance of the absolutely Other. It is with reference to this experience that it is said of the Pharisees that "prostitutes and publicans shall precede them." Because they flee from the prostitutes and publicans, they do not let themselves be caught in the trap. The Pharisees swallow up their "god" and the others, nullifying the function of the others as others—that is to say, their function as critic and summons: "You love the front seats in the synagogues and marks of respect in public." They construct their own little internal opposition, directed and controlled, instead of the denial of self that would force them to come out of their own house. The prostitutes and publicans, on the other hand, clash with a world that rejects them: "We don't want your kind." The Pharisees are prepared to accept all the invectives by which the contradictions in their lifestyle are denounced—its incoherencies in regard to the world—and to accept being judged for not belonging completely to their own system. They weep torrents of tears if it is shown to them that they are not sufficiently and seriously

Pharisees, but they will never tolerate a discussion of how mistaken not only they, but also the Pharisee world, the whole system is. The prostitute and publican are criticized in regard to categories: They could be good, but their condition condemns them. They have no other way out but one of these alternatives: either lock themselves up in a self that is aggressive, with hackles raised, or rise out of the conditioning of the category—to let themselves be looked at and questioned by the Other.

I think that this discovery of the absolutely Other—which is definitive and at the same time new, since it is a living relation of permanent oppositeness—is what we call contemplation, virginity, or the fullness of love.

We try to remake the psychological or historical road on which we have to arrive at the Other, but it is clear that what is involved is the gift of the Other to the self, a liberation that comes to us from outside, an invasion of the Other into the self. This is really the coming of age of the person. I repeat that I see in this the essence of being a Christian. The person is a structure of otherness. We were born to open ourselves to the other. We are lost when we do not find this otherness, and our openness to others is false for being a projection of the self. The real, absolute, incurable unhappiness is loneliness. I identify with Christ as the only Other, the irreducible Other. He can make the gift of himself to the individual under other names, under other symbols. He gave himself to the person long before his name was known on earth, and he continues to give himself to people who do not know him, or who flee from him because the image they have formed of him does not coincide with this absolute Other. I call him Christ Jesus, because he presented himself to me with this name and that is how I understand him.

Liberation is this, liberation from the self, leaving the self to go to the Other, answering the constant call of the Other. It is not a return to Augustinian intimacy because it is precisely concern for others that impels us to search for an otherness that would be real, and the others are one guarantee that we have found the Other. Our point of reference is knowing how to love, and it is for the others to say this. What need is there that love should be chemically pure? What if it is mixed with egoism, hypersensitivity, self-interest, so long as it is love? But a love that is not otherness but a projection of the self augments the micro-macro structure of slavery in the world and accentuates the relationship of oppressed-oppressor. The problem seems to be serious, because just how many arrive at the "one thing necessary," to the discovery of the absolutely Other, and therefore love?

After having talked at length with a nonbeliever—at least that is what she called herself—I asked her to spell out some of her ideas on celibacy. I put down faithfully what she gave me by way of an answer:

I understand celibacy to be a state one arrives at after having gone down a long road of full and deep denials, of painful disengagements. A state one arrives at alone but not in loneliness. A natural being-alone, not self-imposed, without any kind of violence. A state in which loved ones are remembered without a compulsive need for their presence. One is no longer lonely, because he has an immense capacity for communicating with the greatest possible number of people with whom there can be communication. The capacity to live fully every human relationship. The capacity for tenderness is not snuffed out, but rather there is a greater capacity for receiving tenderness from others who are *distinct from us* [I italicize this] and when this tenderness is absent, it becomes bearable through the love we feel and through total surrender to others.

The person who wrote this is thirty-six years old, is married, has given birth to seven children, one of whom died, and has gone through the different stages of love. She describes now a state that is different from hers, from the framework in which she lives as a woman. Her account, like all things that pass the test of living, cannot be identified with a theologically exact definition of the encounter with God, of the contemplative state, of virginity. But it traces some uncertain lines that tell us something about the mystery of the person, something about the reason why the person does not make a pair, nor consequently a community.

Until we feel ourselves thrown into the depths of self, in extreme poverty, and there open ourselves to the absolutely Other, beyond where the "other" is admitted, we will not find the center of unification where the thirst for the Other is slaked in a profound and definitive way, a thirst that is the structural need in all of us. Saint Paul is not falling into rhetoric when he speaks of the "breadth and length and height and depth" (Eph 3, 18) in describing the experience of encounter with Christ. In the experience of this absolutely Other, loneliness is not possible because one is inhabited there where no one else can come; loneliness is not possible because no one else is so complementary, so alike, and at the same time *so opposed to my self, as the Other*. How can we rid ourselves of the temptations to flee, of the desires to abandon a hard and difficult task, which becomes even more arduous through the siren call of comfort, of power, of the betrayal of others, of the desire for peace, of the vision of inefficacy? What form does our "victory" take? It is like an obscure but strong and invincible security that tells me that this commitment, this dream, this hope, which will come true tomorrow, is not a projection of my self, not a fantasy, but a certainty that I receive from "Someone" who transcends me, who is over me and who can impose on my self a "mustness," a "you have to," which can end in death.

Physical solitude, being alone, is necessary, since this presence within us is not static, it is not a little statue we carry within us, it is not a "supernatural" organ that takes shape within us. It is a center of creativity, a painful but joyous dialogue. I don't remember whether it was Braque or another artist who asked his wife, whom he loved profoundly, to leave him alone in his creative moment. It is the moment in which the absolutely Other issues a call to dialogue: the moment from which the most deeply loved person can be excluded, and this exclusion is not possible unless there is absolute freedom and affective maturity. For this reason it is difficult to live with creative people.

At times I ask myself if, on bringing together experiences so disparate, I am falling into a frightening syncretism. But then I think that the One I call Christ Jesus, the Word of God, is so essential to the human structure, so necessary to the history of the person, that there have to be any number of roads along which he can meet us and be Other. He has to be much more "universal" than we can imagine. He is the light that is given to every person *who comes into the world.* Certainly there is the mystery of evil, the choice of darkness, the rejection of the light. We can grasp the mystery only in the "phenomena" of liberty, joy, fullness; of slavery, loneliness, fear of time, and aggressions.

The allusion to a profound and definitive "center of fullness" does not sit well, certainly, with the young generation. "Profound" is out since it is not evident. "Definitive" is out because it reminds them of the spiritual, intellectual, or economic "establishment" that begets hypocrisy and violent persecution. But this center is "profound" because it takes otherness to its furthest consequence—the capacity to make the gift of self to the other, to recognize and to mirror the other as distinct from self. It is not visible, because to perceive what is being lived out deep down can only be attained by the concrete exercise of otherness. Circumstances will not always bring such a person "to lay down his life for his friends," but totally absent from his love for others will be the instrumentalizing, the thingifying, the using of others. Young people feel that the friendship of the "liberated" person is liberating and not dominating. It is definitive because there cannot be one who is more absolutely Other. But for the very reason that he is totally Other, he has to be opposed to my desire to make him captive, to make him mine, to destroy him as a challenge, a provocation, a force making me come out of my self. He is the One who opposes me continually, not to destroy me, but to carry me ever further on, to restrain the repeated attempts of my self to close up and to fold myself into my self.

In the obscure mystery of life we have some guidelines that enable us to verify if we have arrived at Otherness, to see if the irreducibly Other has liberated us—a liberation that is never definitive because one can fall back into slavery. Personally I think that, in the course of time, there ought to come into existence an acquired state, a lasting form of being, even when this state is tormented by continual ups-and-downs. Many of these verifications cannot be made by those living the experience of encounter; the others can do this much better. Therefore, friendship is necessary. We have a need of the others as points of reference to know the mystery of our existence. And the more rich and active existence becomes, the more necessary friendship is. The mark of the friendship of someone who is living the mystery of the encounter with the Other is that of being "necessary" and, therefore, especially solicitous, human, humble. Think about the friendship of the saints, of the true artists, of the people definitely committed to a cause of freedom, of salvation. Think of those commissioned to give the world a message creative of the person, and you will discover the marks of a fragility that is almost childish, of a lowly tenderness, the scars of a wound, the pain of an open sore, which contrasts with the superhuman vigor with which they carry forward and realize their dream.

A control—perhaps the clearest—is "to be alone, without being lonely," which is not a brainy paradox. We cannot fight loneliness; it is perhaps the only sickness for which there will never be a cure. It is the one point at which we will always find need for redemption. I have seen people drug themselves, exhaust themselves heroically, or commit suicide, without achieving a remedy for their loneliness. We can resign ourselves, but resignation because of the lack of something that is absolutely owed to us is an injustice, and little by little it destroys us. This great absence is probably the origin of all our madnesses and aggressions.

To live no longer in loneliness does not mean to have avoided pain. Whoever has found the Other has not avoided the great human cross of time and space. The more total the Other is, the more we suffer from our incapacity. Incapacity in the etymological sense: There is not enough room for you, I cannot contain you: "This treasure we possess in earthen vessels to make it clear that its surpassing power comes from God and not from us" (2 Cor 4, 7). The suffering *of time*, because the Other, being always beyond, obliges us to come out: There is no arrival point except in hope. Those who say that the person of faith is one who has avoided anguish and uncertainties don't know what they are talking about. If he were raised immediately to this state of being without a preliminary experience of trials, doubts, of "painful disengagements," I don't think he could stand it.

The Beatitudes are a test of liberation. If we take this famous page as a sign of liberation achieved, it would be idle to ask ourselves if it is obligatory for all or just for a small Christian elite. It is the test of the liberated self, and therefore is to be found in the common destiny of the person. It is the person open to the other "definitively" and, at the same time, anchored in the definitive, in the permanent. It is "conservation" rescued from altruism; it is altruism made real, full, authentic, by conservation. This last is an altered truth, an idea lost, a line developed exaggeratedly. We are not altruists if we are not conservers, and we are not conservers if we are not open to the Other and to the others. The paradox is expressed in the gospel phrase that we often use without giving it its full meaning: "The man who loves his life loses it, while the man who hates his life in this world preserves it to life eternal" (Jn 12, 25). And we find it above all in the maxim that fuses supreme egoism with supreme altruism: "You shall love . . . your neighbor as yourself" (Lk 10, 27).

The "conservative" line of the Beatitudes is demanding. The conservers take it as a joke, as a fraud: "Happy are those who are poor in spirit," that is to say, those who do not cover up their existential insufficiency with money, with goods, with things, with "thingified" persons. Happy are those who discover with joy their insufficiency, because it opens them to the Other and to the others. Happy are those who are sad because they cannot enjoy the Other right away, and hence suffer the pain of time and space. Happy are those who have a pure and humble heart, that is, those who refuse to clutter it up with power and things, keeping it open to the Other.

Along the line of otherness there is discovered a permanent hunger for justice, for complete justice, the increasing and restless work for peace that never ends in victory. A beautiful text of Pannenberg says: "Peace is a provisional state of justice recognized unanimously by the interested sides. And given that the situation is always provisional, peace is always 'for the moment.' " Thus is revealed compassion for the others, for all those who suffer, a compassion which is a sharing of the effort to search for liberating joy. Thus is revealed the self open to the Other, ready to accept persecution and death in order not to lose this opening. Those who live this experience live it in such a veiled and ambiguous way that they cannot "feel like liberated people." Now and then we receive some ambivalent and incomplete sign, some spark, that helps us to face up to the risk of living.

If I were to say to the person I have quoted that she is on the road to liberation because she has found Otherness—that is, the One that she does not recognize, that she does not name even though perhaps she feels him, lives him—she probably would not believe me. And yet the signs are there, despite her not seeing them. If Otherness could be seen in a fixed and certain way, it would cease to be such, because the movement to get outside the self would immediately become paralyzed through the satisfaction of something accomplished, of something possessed. The remembrance with joy of people one loves, without an accompanying and anguished need to see them, to possess them, is only possible if the person is indwelt and not in loneliness. To love without possessing, without the anguish of the shipwreck victim who clings to the other as a plank of salvation, is proper to whoever is open to the absolutely Other. The capacity to give tenderness grows out of the capacity to receive tenderness.

There are no lives surrounded only by barbed wire, people who only get kicked about and rebuffed. God surrounded us with the tenderness of things, of the world, so that although we should find only hardened faces and closed doors, we would discover a tenderness sweeter and more secure because it would not depend on attitudes or on economic or racial classifications. This tenderness of the world is not always discovered or experienced. We are not talking about esthetic emotion, which is pleasure. Tenderness is something else. It is the fullness of life that enters into us, the cosmic joy of living, because we feel ourselves to be within a plan thought out in love. To give tenderness is easy because the deeply wounded person looks for all possible occasions to offer it. On the other hand, to receive it is *more difficult;* it presupposes all we have said above. We often come across people who think they love very much, who see themselves as super-producers of love, and who complain of receiving only a pittance in return. I have often been disturbed by these unfortunates who never manage to collect on the very important titles they have in their hands. But then I discovered that their history is empty of love and that the root cause of the evil lies in their incapacity for receiving tenderness.

The woman whose note I quoted earlier on knows the caress of hands, the kiss on the mouth, the embrace of the body, and speaks for those of us who have renounced the physical embrace but not tenderness; because those who cannot accept tenderness are not human. They may be robots capable of transmitting words and orders and the like, but they are not people. If I had written what she wrote, I would be regarded as living on abstractions, projecting erotic reality on images. I would be considered sick. The importance of this woman's note lies in its expression of a concrete, vivid, carnal experience of love.

I have allowed myself to correct this phrase: "not pairing off with anyone"—in order to pair off with all. What is meant, I believe, is that the love she is writing about has nothing to do with neutrality toward people—all equal, all loved with the same love. That would be an abstraction which would reduce itself to anti-love. She lives and feels all kinds of love which undoubtedly have different degrees, free from possessiveness and egoism. It is clear how a man and woman can love each other exclusively and at the same time remain open to others and love them; a love which the others see as "diverse" but equally full, total, exclusive, and different for each person. Perhaps this is the trait that makes us most like God.

I want to emphasize once more this "capacity" for receiving

tenderness, for being accepted. If a person who had not lived authentically in liberation had composed those lines for me, aided only by logic and intuition, the text would have read "the capacity to give tenderness to all." For me this is the most important and revolutionary intuition in the gospel: The sign that Saint Francis has discovered God, the true God and not an idol, the absolutely Other, should be looked for not in his daring and valiant commitment to follow Christ in poverty and suffering, but in his feeling of being enveloped in the tenderness of the world. Contemplatives, hermits, should comfort people not with words but with a life that the others ought to find surrounded by tenderness. "Their harmonious relations and joyful faces," as Dante said of the first Franciscan community, show that an existential, profound Other exists without whom all the others can come to be only a horrid camouflage of the self through which we never arrive at eliminating the terrifying loneliness of life. Celibacy is a tremendous challenge, a gigantic act of faith, because if the Other does not come to me and dwell in me I remain stretched out toward the others and toward things like a shipwrecked person reaching for a plank.

If it could be understood that Christians—not those who follow Christian morality and practice, not those who go to the temple and mechanically repeat the formulas of the *Credo*, but those who accept Christ and live his adventure—are more necessary to the world than any other type of creator, there would rise up from the earth a great outcry from all people for the Other that I call the Lord Jesus. There is a familiar cretinous and sentimental axiom that goes like this: How beautiful the world would be if only we would do a little more good, if only we were more Christian, more like brothers and sisters to one another! The phrase is obscene when it is uttered by bejeweled people, wallowing in comfort, who only want to dispel from their blue heaven the little clouds of antipathy that surround them. It is certain that if only we would love each other more, everything would be resolved: If the United States would only love Latin America and the Orient, if bishops would only love their priests, if the tenants of apartment 12 would only love the tenants of apartment 13, if husbands would only love their wives, all would be resolved. But we have got to begin with the recognition that we do not know how to love. I think I love. I seem to love, I am under the illusion of loving, but I do not know how to love. I possess, I destroy, I deform. I use, I do not love. I discover this in a certain hidden sourness, in the depths of an insatiable sadness. It is the feeling that someone owes me something, that someone is withholding *what is mine.*

The parable of the laborers (Mt 20, 1–16) figures in the picture of this sadness. The one who gripes is the one who sees his relationship with the Other as a contract, and he has the impression that the Other has cheated him, that the boss is a "hard and cruel" man. He who has found the Other to be an absolute necessity for his person, a reason for living, is satisfied. Satisfied and, at the same time, with the lacerating sadness of receiving too much, of "not knowing where to put, what to do with, all that." This sadness can be more difficult to bear than the other, that of "having received too little"; it can be so unbearable as to carry us to the extreme, what is called "to die of love," which is not in the least rhetorical or imaginary. On the other hand, the sadness of feeling cheated generates a bourgeois, lukewarm, resigned atmosphere, compensated by things so worthless that one feels ashamed of belonging to the human species.

The repose of Mary, who receives the word, and through the word the Other, is the most exact picture of being alone and yet not being lonely. But can one arrive at this repose without suffering and without a painful experience of love? The fact that we are all structurally designed for "otherness," that we cannot live without the other, often drives us to look for easy solutions. The other is too accessible, too near, too attractive, for us to lose time in reflection. We must experience an absolute necessity in order to arrive at receiving the absolutely Other, and consequently at being received by the others. A Protestant version of the Beatitudes translates the first one in this way: "Happy are those who have a spiritual need." This is an exact translation of evangelical poverty, as long as it is not taken superficially. It is the necessity without remedy—without our being able to telephone a friend, the Jesuit father, or a psychiatrist. The only exit door to the Other is total poverty, with no possibility for salvation and suicide the only escape. Therefore "poor in spirit" would mean poor in love, incapable, not accepted, rejected. The stupid question, Do you mean poor in spirit or sociological poverty? would no longer have any meaning. Those who dwell in large convents, the owners of huge stock holdings, now have found a way to practice poverty without losing anything: to accuse subversive priests of practicing a "sociological poverty." If they would only read the Song of Songs one more time, they would be ashamed of their petty bourgeois habits and stop walking off their boredom along the beautiful, shaded corridors of the convent, reading psalms that have lost their meaning. "On my bed at night I sought him whom my heart loves—I sought him but I did not find him. . . . The watchmen came upon me as they made their rounds of the city. Have you seen him whom my heart loves?" (Sgs 3, 1–3).

To think about poverty, apart from this search for otherness, without having accepted the Other, is to waste time. If the truly poor could be present at one of our religious "chapters" in which we discuss the topic of poverty, they would look at us with eyes full of alarm, surprise, and amusement, as though we were specimens of an absolutely unknown species. The poor are those, and only those, who have discovered, painfully, that if we are not loved and accepted, life—even when it is full of events and comforts—is death. Because of all this, to think about poverty within the framework of privilege, without our thought arising from a real interior need, but only so that our lifestyle will not be scandalous and cause criticism, is simply sacrilegious. To be received is the only truly human, essential, indispensable thing and the only thing in the face of which every one of us is helpless. We cannot understand the Other and let him dwell within us so long as we do not live extensively in this situation of rejection, of loneliness. It is the theme of Zacchaeus, of Levi, of the prodigal son, of Mary. For me poverty is not optional; it is essential in the encounter with Christ. Certainly one can live in this situation even in opulence; indeed it is easier for this feeling of "emptiness," of loneliness, of distaste, to be born out of wealth than out of poverty—in the same way that it is easier for one involved in love affairs to feel the need for love than it is if our life is devoid of love. But the rich man is tempted to use the means at hand to resolve his problem with successive, provisional solutions.

Next, as a sign of having really discovered the Other, as a consequence of an otherness truly of the spirit, there ought to be a new attitude about things: They have no finality in the self but are a bridge to friendship. I always distrust conversions that do not revolutionize life. Otherness should not be a marginal acquisition; it should become the law of life, the only and exclusive reason for living. When changes, impoverishments, are coldly decided by decree, the Holy Spirit is offended. It is necessary to shout at the top of our voice in the church today: "Do not sadden the Holy Spirit." It is necessary to have the courage to ask, like Mary before the empty tomb: "Tell me, where have you put him?" This is the real problem; poverty comes later. The non-poverty and our casuistic ability to "adapt" poverty is the proof, the clearest indication, that we don't know where the Other is. We blame the young generation for wanting a Christ without the church, a gospel cut off from the ecclesial tradition, but we should have the courage to admit that *our* church is without Christ, empty.

Poverty does not exist; the poor exist, those whom society excludes from the enjoyment of good things. These things are reserved for those who have a legal right to them. And there are also the voluntarily poor, those who have stripped themselves since the encounter with the Other. The encounter with the essential instantly empties and drains the color from what seemed to be essential. It permanently revolutionizes life; it changes radically the sense of "personal rotation." Hitherto the others revolved around me, now it is my self that revolves around the others. I am reminded once again of the "rule" in poverty that Father de Foucauld left us:

My God, I do not know how it is possible for some souls to see you poor and yet remain voluntarily rich, to see themselves greater than their Teacher, than their dearly Beloved. In any case I cannot conceive of love without a need, an imperious need, to conform one's life to his, to be like him and to share all the pain, the difficulties and hardships of life (*Oeuvres spirituelles*, p. 520).

It is always objected that the ecclesial structures must be so large and practical as to receive both those who have already found the Other and those who have not found him. Therefore it is necessary to think about poverty from the outside, in a poor structure in which all could live. Unfortunately, a religious structure is so vast, so bourgeois, that in the search for the Other it is more of an obstacle than an effective help. I believe that its style, its manner of being, ought to be discovered by those who have found the Other. Only in this way could it be attractive to those who begin to suspect that otherness is the only reason for living, and that, along this road, otherness is definitely to be discovered. If religious life comes to this—which is its only meaning, its only reason for existing, the "discovering of the Other," the only and definitive foundation for all otherness—and begins to look from this angle at poverty, chastity, relationship with things and persons, it will still have a charter of citizenship in the world. If not, it should have the courage to recognize its absolute uselessness.

The road is certainly risky, because coming out of the self is a new emergence from the womb, more perilous and more painful than the former. We are capable of all kinds of heroics as long as we can avoid this "coming out of self." We fight like titans to suppress the opposition, the other, that which questions us and resists us. We flee from otherness. Pain is the only force that can make us accept it. The wounded body of Christ, totally open to the Other and delivered to us who are the "others," is the sign of the history of each of us. I think about the loneliness of Job and of Christ and about the innumerable human histories that repeat, from vicissitude to vicissitude, the same history. It is worth noting how much people like to hear stories about this dear old monk or that nun who in their youth had a love affair that ended in disillusionment. These cheap fantasies have often irritated me; they hand us such a trivial *Love Story*. But isn't there something real underneath this popular passion? Can we come to the Other without a disillusionment in love? The history of Christ is a history of disillusionment. It is the history of one who offered himself to the others, who was not understood, who was betrayed: "To his own he came. Yet his own did not accept him" (Jn 1,11). Love is not only that which is sung about with guitar accompaniment under a full moon or that is danced to in a night club. That of Christ is a love without illusions, rejected.

Can we open ourselves to the Other without the pain of having been previously rejected in our attempt to give ourselves to the others, without having suffered it in our own flesh, without knowing loneliness? I think of the old doctor in a Bergman film who futilely hopes, in the loneliness of his oncoming death, to "be accepted" by the governess who had served him faithfully for many years. He would like to be spoken to as an equal and to enter as "other" into her life. But she will not accept him. Perhaps through this relationship of discovering the Other in pain and love, we can identify the woman of Luke's Gospel with Mary Magdalen and the sinful woman. Three women in one. Because Mary Magdalen would not have searched so desperately for the dead Christ if he had not been Other for her, and Mary would not have acquired this capacity to become lost at the feet of the Master, listening to him, if she had not been disillusioned by the others. Only pain can make us discover helplessness and poverty.

But neither is pain infallible. Between the saints and the despairing ones, the "suicides," is the middle class of resignation: Those who are content with their happiness. Few drops of love were given us, but there are women, cars, buildings, stockholdings. It is the drama of freedom: We can reject God. The cross is the ultimate invention, the desperate cry that the Other hurls at the person. This clarifies a little the esteem that physically handicapped people, with an enduring destiny for suffering, as well as contemplatives, have always enjoyed in "Christendom." It is said that those who suffer are a visible actualization of Christ crucified, and that they suffer for our sins. But it would be monstrous to think that God would avenge himself on this person for the sins I have committed, even more monstrous when this person would accept it lovingly. I want none of it.

But inasmuch as these wounded people open themselves to the Other, they become guides to lead me along the one road that I also have to travel, even though my history would be different. The history that is hidden in me becomes, in these people, a model, a sign in their own bodies, and therefore has a mysterious influence on me.

The contemplative shows us the point of arrival. It is not because of a sick love for suffering and victimism or a flight from the "action" that people have always felt a mysterious attraction toward those martyred in the body and toward contemplatives, two useless categories. The search for otherness is basically our true occupation. Our great sufferings and the periods of real rest, the breathing spells that pump oxygen into our existence, are episodes in this history. Episodes also are the violence, the gift of self, the rejection and the acceptance. Contemplatives keep the root of our otherness uncovered. They are persons whom events, vocation, and their particular makeup and, above all, suffering have thrust to the depths of their selves. And there they live, living nevertheless the life of all. Everyone would like to arrive there, and in fact we must arrive there, so that our otherness and the meaning of life will be genuine. The person who suffers in the flesh becomes a sacrament, a sign of the road that leads to this root, just like Christ crucified "outside the gates," excluded from the community.

There is no other destiny for us, for any of us. Mary has arrived at the "definitive" thing that nothing or nobody will take from her.

8

She Who Was Not Invited

There was a certain Pharisee who invited Jesus to dine with him. Jesus went to the Pharisee's home and reclined to eat. A woman known in the town to be a sinner learned that he was dining in the Pharisee's home. She brought in a vase of perfumed oil and stood behind him at his feet, weeping so that her tears fell upon his feet. Then she wiped them with her hair, kissing them and perfuming them with the oil.

When his host, the Pharisee, saw this, he said to himself, "If this man were a prophet, he would know who and what sort of woman this is that touches him—that she is a sinner."

In answer to his thoughts, Jesus said to him, "Simon, I have something to propose to you."

"Teacher," he said, "speak."

"Two men owed money to a certain money-lender; one owed a total of five hundred coins, the other fifty. Since neither was able to repay, he wrote off both debts. Which of them was more grateful to him?"

Simon answered, "He, I presume, to whom he remitted the larger sum."

Jesus said to him, "You are right."

Turning then to the woman, he said to Simon: "You see this woman? I came to your home and you provided me with no water for my feet. She has washed my feet with her tears and wiped them with her hair. You gave me no kiss, but she has not ceased kissing my feet since I entered. You did not anoint my head with oil, but she has anointed my feet with perfume. I tell you, that is why her many sins are forgiven—because of her great love. Little is forgiven the one whose love is small."

He said to her then, "Your sins are forgiven"; at which his fellow

167

guests began to ask among themselves, "Who is this that he even forgives sins?"

Meanwhile he said to the woman, "Your faith has been your salvation. Now go in peace" (Lk 7, 36–50).

The itinerary of this woman seems to be the archetype of history: the emergence of the person from an undifferentiated plurality. The woman emerges wordless, but with many gestures of love, in the cold, inhospitable dining room before two men. The one is responsible for her fall into plurality, into non-identity; the other calls her to oneness, to identity. The woman in Luke's gospel is an argument against the pharisaical kind of wealth—self-sufficiency and spiritual security. Only the woman can break down the objectivized security that the law gives in order to choose the other security that is deep, intimate, unattainable for one who is not looking for a special acceptance: the security that the person offers. In the battle against the economic security and self-sufficiency that money and possessions afford, Christ is at the head of the poor, of those condemned to be left behind. In the fight against the Pharisees—doctrinal security, spriritual self-sufficiency—he is all for the woman.

The Samaritan woman, the adulteress, Mary Magdalen, the sister of Martha, the Canaanite woman, the woman who bursts into the house of Simon—all have a profound oneness. They give a name, a body, and a history to the polemic against self-sufficiency, against the security that comes from outside as a privilege. Christ's conversation with the Samaritan woman breaks open the visible and material boundaries of the "kingdom": God is beyond the temple of Jerusalem and the mountain of Samaria. The adulteress is exempted from the implacable law, because human beings are called to a self-awareness that antedates the law and is above it. Mary Magdalen is sent to announce the resurrection as the meaning and substance of the entire gospel. Mary discovers the Other and is made one; that is, she is brought back from the diaspora of "many things" to concentrate on the one thing necessary. The Canaanite woman breaks through the rigid frontier of privilege, and through the encounter with the man enters into the kingdom community. The uninvited woman at Simon's house discovers the human relationship as "emergence" after having experienced encounter with men as promiscuity and diaspora. They all prove the uselessness of the law, and they search for security in interpersonal relationship. Woman is much more insecure than man because the kinds of "security" that man has provisionally going for him scarcely exist for the woman. She stakes everything on the person, gambles with her destiny, and invests her wealth in the person. Therefore, she is poorer, more often betrayed and disillusioned, than man. But at the same time she is more confident of salvation, richer in hope, more attentive to the message of the person. On this poverty Christ bases his war against the security that is illusory in that it is external to people, not part of their history.

Simon, the Pharisee, belongs to the group of men who condemn the woman in the public square and make her an adulteress in the dark. Christ's awesome gaze astounds them; it has somewhat the fascination and terror of an apparition. They have no time nor freedom to defend themselves—"Let the man among you who has no sin be the first to cast a stone at her." Straightening up unexpectedly, he makes them back away as if driven by whips. He does not set out to argue about the law, to demand proofs, or to ask compassion for the woman taken in adultery. Christ does not go with the poor to beg at the doors of the rich: he goes with them to accuse and denounce. He does not defend the adulteress with an interpretation of the law, he asks no favors. He takes the woman's side and accuses the male. And he does not do so by seeking to excuse the woman on the grounds of her "weakness"; he denounces the relationship by putting himself on the victim's side. It is not a question of two equal opponents; it is a question of an injustice involving everybody, one which should be considered and confronted from the perspective of the one who suffers the injustice, even though the fact of the oppression soils the virtue of the victim. Woe to you rich, for you will be judged by the poor! Woe to you men, for you will be judged by women! The Pharisee casts the woman out into the darkness, where she has no identity—where she is only a body, a caress, flesh, pleasure. And so that she will not rise up and appear in the banquet hall demanding a seat at table, he casts her out beyond the barrier of the law. Nobody is as much applauded, as well-paid, as desirable as woman provided that she is called a star, a queen, a mother—titles that designate her in terms of function, not as the "thou" or "other" of man. Money and women are the two closed rings in which man circles around. They represent the tight space of the prisoner that the absolutely Other has not been able to liberate. And the wall that protects this space we call power, law, tradition, fear.

The adulteress, desired and possessed in the night, is condemned in the sunlit square. The other who appears at Simon's house, though known in the darkness, is not accepted in the light. If this man were truly a prophet, he would know what kind of woman is touching him. We are dealing here with a person who leads a bad life. He, Simon, knows her; but not here, where the guests have a name, an identity. For her there is no other destiny: from desire to repudiation, from the lustful and depersonalized embrace to the "I don't know you." It is the whole story of identity, denied to the poor by the rich and denied to the woman by the Pharisee.

At a meeting in this valley, I met a woman of the neighborhood who had five children by four different men. A lady present—legally married and a practicing Catholic—insolently addressed her as "Miss." One of the former woman's children, a fifteen-year-old boy, is a slave—that is the precise word—in this lady's house. He works round the clock every day, with only a little break on Sunday afternoon. He is paid six dollars a month—that is, six dollars worth of groceries for the mother. Both the boy and the mother are victims of male power. The law is a safeguard against infection from the two of them: the woman is a "prostitute," a "bad woman"; the unfortunate boy is "subversive." The law prohibits them from emerging from their condition, for every attempt to do so is labeled subversive. Christ turns the situation upside down, making the victims into the saviors. He places in their hands a power that the development of history and human thought try tirelessly to understand to make effective. The totality of this power, the fullness of the decisions, will be evident with the coming of the kingdom. Every movement of history is an unfolding of this power that belongs as a right to the oppressed and is in practice denied them. To us who live in time, this movement appears only as a correction of the cruelty of this power or as a simple changing of the guard.

The Christian community must anticipate "global history" in the world and transmit to this history its upward thrust. The meaning of Christian communities, and therefore of the church, is to keep alive and operative in history a picture of the kind of world we are headed for and for which we are painfully searching. Christ draws the man-woman relationship out of the juridical schema of the Pharisees. He already sees the liberated relationship, because the victims will transcend the sinful, erroneous relationship and discover the true relationship in love, a relationship stripped of power, of self-interest, of egoism. The woman who enters Simon's house does not judge man or forgive him; she *accepts* him. Judgment and forgiveness belong to our space; acceptance is within the space of love. The two spaces are not intercommunicable; they are parallel. Of ourselves we can arrive at remorse, at forgiveness, but not at the kind of love that means rebirth.

I cannot continue without dealing with a statement made to me by an atheist friend for whom I have great respect and love: "We feel as if we were profoundly understood and have the sense of doing a good stretch of the road together, but after that you leave us at a crossroads and go intrepidly on your journey." But, my friend, can one arrive at a new relationship, at a new, true love—at acceptance—without a rebirth, without a rebuilding which takes place inside us but does not come from ourselves? By "acceptance" I mean a relationship in which there is no room for domination nor subordination nor vengeance, nor even less for forgiveness as we understand it when we think: the past remains, but I—I who am so good —don't keep it in mind. It is easy to demonstrate that hypocrisy and caste distinctions and any other sort of oppression can insinuate themselves into what very well might seem to be a really sublime act of a person. Is it perhaps possible that we can never really rid ourselves of the categories in terms of which we see and regulate all our relationships? This is the great question on which the all-or-nothing of faith depends. I don't want to abandon you, my friend, nor can I pretend that you accept my hypothesis. I know it will seem too facile to you, too superficial and, underneath, frozen stiff with fear. We can still go on together united in the same sad notion that love is actually impossible for us. But I cannot hide from you the fact that I see included in our history the hope of this possibility. I would not tell you this if the One in whom I believe as the hope of history had not bound up this hope with humiliation, defeat, death.

Simon and the woman belong to two different worlds, to two different "galaxies." The sinful man who has looked upon the woman lustfully now becomes her judge: If you only knew the kind of woman who is touching you. But the woman is on another plane. She is not the one "received," she is the one who *receives*. She does not forgive, she accepts. It is symptomatic that Christ defines her gestures of love as acceptance. Simon has not received her although he is the owner of the house. The banquet is at his expense, he has taken the initiative of inviting the Lord. He has tried to put on a pleasant dinner, but in fact he did not receive the guest. Simon is sitting next to his guest physically, but he is not in the latter's space. He is enclosed by the circle of the law and of self-sufficiency. She who receives Christ is not the owner of the house but an intruder. Christ spells out the acceptance shown in the loving gestures of hospitality. "I came to your home and you provided me with no water for my feet. She has washed my feet with her tears and wiped them with her hair. You gave me no kiss, but she has not ceased kissing my feet since I entered. You did not anoint my head with oil, but she has anointed my feet with perfume." She has received me in a house that is not hers, and you have not received me. I would like to say to my atheist friend that this profound poverty unites us: I know the house of the Son of Man, I know that it is there; but maybe I have not received him in fact. I don't know how many encounters, how many "acceptances," are present in today's harlequinesque search, symbolized in *Godspell,* as well as in the desire to bring about justice with methods that issue only in violence. And instead of acceptances, how many rebuffs are produced in the house where he has been officially and pompously invited by those who feel secure and proud of sitting next to him? It is well to think, now and then, that he could be in our house and that we have not received him.

The discourse of Christ to Simon can be summed up in this way: She has received me in a house not hers, and you have not received me in yours. The woman receives him because she has found the "thou," and she has found him in the very act of receiving him. "Make friends of the poor so that they will receive you in their homes." The poor woman *receives* the Son of Man. She who is used to submitting herself to the erotic desires of men receives exquisitely the guest who was not received. Now she takes the initiative of kissing and caressing, the real initiative that she had never taken even when she was pleasing men with her caresses. She returns to man the gestures she had received, not to wreak vengeance, within the tragic schema of domination, but as a sign of liberation. Her gestures, even though she might not think so, are objectively a judgment on the male. The very acts of love have betrayed her because they were an expression of the seductive and dominating male. And in the same erotic ambience, she has repeated them, giving them the same meaning of seduction and domination. Now she reconstructs them with the opposite meaning of relationship and love; now they express the coming out of the self, the going to the other. Alongside the man of the law, who has no doubts about himself and his rights, emerges the liberated woman. And the sign of her liberation is the new meaning her gestures of love have acquired.

We have nothing more than our bodies to express relationship, and with the very same signs we express both eroticism and love. The woman invents another sign—perfume. Her perfume is "her"—her presence, her call, the power of attraction with which she has always remained in slavery, alternately happy and despairing, satisfied and empty. Eroticism has continually renewed in her the surprise of love; every adventure is a new beginning. She has lived every encounter as a surprise, whereas for the male it has been something physiological. She sees every adventure as a hope and a search. The male goes to her attracted by her aroma, with desire but without hope, since the law is his protection and will defend him. Just the way he goes down to the poor to give and, perhaps, receive a fleeting emotion, a sadistic pleasure, a mixture of the oppressor's remorse and the satisfaction of one who bestows largesse. Something that is like sexual pleasure, mixed with degradation. He does not go down to the poor to be received. And no male approaches her to be received: All come to possess her. And each one revives in her the hope of discovering a poor person, homeless, excluded. Finally she finds him: "You have not washed my feet, and she has done nothing but bathe them with her tears." Christ makes the Samaritan woman feel the same thing. He, a Jew, asks her for a drink of water. Present in the world, he is not received, present in the house of Simon, he is not received. It is evident that to pretend to take sides does not do away with oppression. The oppressed who goes over to the side of power is the oppressor; woman, endowed with the power of man, oppresses in turn. It is necessary to turn oppression into acceptance. And is it possible for us to achieve this by relying only on our own strengths?

The other three evangelists speak of a similar episode: the anointing at Bethany. It is not of much interest whether this is the same episode or not. One can indeed inquire into this other "unction" to determine what meaning the very same actions have. Woman consecrates man with the identical rite kings and priests are consecrated with, recognizing in the man seated at the table the "thou" that frees her from slavery. History will produce agreements, laws, cultures that will modify the fundamental man-woman relationship, archetype of all human relationships, but this slow clarification of the relationship will never bring about a love relationship free of possessiveness, aggression, fear.

In the response of Jesus there is a strange change of direction away from the traditional parallelism of Semitic discourse. Whoever receives more, loves more. You would immediately expect a complementary line: She loves much, she loves more than you, because the sins she has been forgiven are more serious than yours. Nevertheless, Jesus says that much is forgiven her because she has loved much. Also this phrase places the woman outside the reach of "pharisaical accountability." Into her love there has crept a demand, a search, a thirst for the person. The woman has not sought to "be perfect" by measuring her life against the law. She has searched for love and the "thou" without finding them. Her body —instrument for communication, of escape from her self, the only means of liberation, abused violently by the other —weighs ever more heavily upon her. Her body, not open to the other but used, not received but taken violently and afterwards abandoned, seals off her loneliness ever more harshly.

For the Pharisee the life of this woman is sin, transgression of the law. She is the excluded one, the one who should not be received in the home. Christ sees her search for the "thou." She, the violated one, the victim, must refashion the relationship. The tears, the hair, the perfume, are the signs with which she reveals her body as a means of establishing herself. We "spiritualists" have failed for centuries to understand the meaning of the caresses with which woman rediscovers the body of man. In the body of man she rediscovers her own as a means of communication and dialogue. The gospel gives us a significant detail: her loving attention to the body of Christ. "Since she came in, she has not ceased to cover my feet with her kisses! The perfume with which she had attracted man hovers around her still. Man leaves afterwards, leaving to her the condemnation. In man the fleeting dominion reinforces his sense of power, and this power is the woman's condemnation: "If you only knew what kind of woman this is." The law of Moses orders this kind of woman to be stoned. I have run into this sort of thing time and again in the rural towns of Latin America. The father is seized with despair when he discovers that his daughter, still a child, is going to be a mother; but he does not say a word against the man, to whom he is bound in an unspoken complicity. She is the one responsible for the deed that dishonors the family.

The woman in the house of Simon does not attract the man with her perfume; she surrounds him with it. It emanates from this woman who is emerging from her state of oppression and is wafted toward the man, not to attract him but "to consecrate him unto death"—to prepare him for the gift of self that will be the salvation of all. She envelops the man, the body that she lovingly discovers, not to possess it but to give it. Because she is received she receives it. The meaning of "receiving" becomes clearer little by little: to love deeply without possessing, to know intimately in order to keep alive the only meaning of life, which is to make the gift of oneself for others. The woman's tears do not express sorrow but a response to the great thing that will never happen again, because no one will ever again be so totally and definitively Other for the woman as Simon's house guest. The rest of us will have to look for him in symbols in the poor, in the community; but no encounter will ever be like this woman's encounter. Jesus says: "The poor you will always have with you but you will not always have me." The phrase authorizes some people—whose stupidity I will not comment on—to deduce that we will always have the poor and that therefore it is useless to try to wipe out poverty. The meaning seems clear to me: The encounter is unrepeatable because this unique man will never again be present in his body or in his words to re-present the model of relationship that the groaning of history cries out for. If the woman had appeared at the door and had not caressed the body of the man for so long and so chastely, the liberation would not have had so clear a meaning. She is not saved and regenerated in an abstract sense: It is her body which is remade, regenerated, rediscovered.

She is *unsatisfied*, and therefore she is outside the enclosure of the Pharisees. Jesus could not be understood by the nicely married and satisfied woman who has resigned herself to the fact that the world has no room for more love, or a different love, than what keeps her going. Mary is the proletarian who is aware of being used, possessed, and is convinced that this is not the human condition. "In the beginning it was not so." The "she loved much" is this awareness, this kindling of hope; it is her rebellion against a servitude that does not have to be. The polemic against the pharisaical world, which is the world of satisfaction, could not be more evident. The law produces the type of the self-satisfied man and therefore is incapable of liberating us since it cannot force us out of the circle of our own selves. Remorse or satisfaction: the two are equivalent in the sense that neither can be the means of emerging from the self. Remorse for having failed to observe the law or satisfaction in having observed it: in either case the self remains locked up in its cage, where it now despairs and now struts, alternating moments of depression with moments of exaltation. But its language, its expression, cannot escape the limits within which it is inevitably circumscribed. If the woman's tears were tears of repentance, they would not be the focus of this polemic against the Pharisees. "She loved much" because she expected something and someone who would make her come out of her self.

The encounter in Simon's house uncovers the most hidden meaning of redemption: Peace is the man-woman relationship saved from the owner-slave, exploiter-exploited pattern. The liberated woman liberates man and consecrates him to the gift of self, with the design of the kingdom, the design of making men more human, more brotherly. This is what is symbolized by her perfume and her loving care for the body of the man. She takes unto herself that body not to hold onto it but to give it. Continually rejecting herself, cast aside as an erotic object already sullied, she now discovers the true direction of her life, the life that now goes out to the Other and the others. Would this not be the meaning of the words said to Mary Magdalene at the tomb: "Do not touch me"? The phrase perhaps will go on being ambiguous and obscure as long as we do not arrive at the heart of the mystery of relationship. Woman either holds onto man, possesses him, or she consecrates him to the others, that is, destines him to a mission, to a community, to history. In any case, *to death*. Either the useless, sterile death of one imprisoned within himself—the island death, the base of Bergman films—or death under the open sky, the death of the others, fecund death because it bears life within itself. Thinking about the gospel, I have asked myself time and again if the commitment made by the revolutionaries in Latin America does not have its origin, although this could seem absurd, in the need to defend the couple. Those young people risk their lives on purpose, not out of boredom but to save their love. They have sensed that in the bourgeois family, so firmly molded by the conservative spirit, the least that is preserved is love. Thus, many young people rediscover, in a vital way, the meaning of the gospel maxim: "He who would save his life must lose it." I am convinced that the new couple will be born, not in dissertations or seminars on love and the family, but *at the barricades.*

The "do not touch me" could be understood in relation to the "anointing, the consecration for death." He who says this has risen above the moment, he is no longer in history, and the woman no longer has the mission to consecrate him for death. Liberation is always the capacity to give life, to come out of self to that last surrender, which is to give oneself in death. Woman enters into this rhythm when she is liberated, that is, not thingified, not possessed, but a partner in man's creativity.

The women in the gospel are seen, with a unique coherence, as totality. Their history is the history of the person; it is the history of their body. Man plays with goods. His history is "economic" and "political" history. The history of woman is constituted by her being woman and the way in which the encounter with man makes her to be woman. This distinction is not so neat and schematic in real life, and every woman would deny being "personal history," as opposed to a history projected beyond the self. In spite of this, the man of today is searching for the origins and the meaning of communication, and he lingers over the interchange of symbols: words, goods, and women. The relationship is emerging from that first "thingification," from the identification of the woman as a negotiable thing, to her personification, to the discovery of the feminine "thou." Between Mary the adulteress, the sister of

Martha, and the woman in Simon's house, whatever the historical identity of each one, there is an undeniable affinity. The alternative is one of all for all. She is not interested in the pharisaic problem, the fierce fight to occupy the seats up front, the fear and discouragement in the face of failure, the whole plot in which men, who feel they are the actors of history, are imprisoned. Her silence in Simon's house is significant.

Woman's liberation is totally a matter of encounter with the other. In the discovery of the "thou" she finds the meaning of her body, of her person. The woman of the perfume has been a prisoner, has been possessed, having lost sight of the meaning of her body. But now rediscovered, remade, she once more finds this meaning, which is the meaning of existence. I think we lose our sense of the body as the ultimate symbol of our reality along two roads: losing ourselves in the spirit and losing ourselves in the flesh. We must rediscover it as symbol and as a means of relationship. But when it is truly rediscovered, we can no longer distract ourselves, taking it for ourselves. We must lose it. The movement that goes from the man to the woman is a movement of domination, of possession; the woman must turn it around. She has the mission of "discovery"—the body of the man, his meaning, his raison d'être. Without this point of departure, without its being well rooted in one's own identity, all the other relationships will fall short. Upon observing how the man who says he is virtuous and religious uses things and shows himself to be insensitive to people, one can only infer that he is blind, that he thinks he sees and touches, but he does not see or touch. He moves in a world of appearances like the man in Plato's cave. Because he has not discovered himself, he lives outside himself.

It is true that the history of woman seems more "dependent," less open to free and personal options. Nevertheless, on the "option" man makes of her depends the future course of history. And this endangered history does not change even when the woman is free to choose the man, to take the initiative. In fact, although the woman apparently waits for the initiative of the man, she is the one who chooses: "Your desire will bring you to your husband." The one who chooses, even though people might have the opposite impression, is the woman, her perfume. But the sequence in time is not so important, because if neither of the two are liberated by the encounter with the Other, it is impossible to avoid the repetition of the tyranny-oppression pattern.

Woman will not know how to find anything more hers, more real, than the movement of Mary: "I am the servant of the Lord. Let it be done to me as you say." The most profound movement by man will be to "leave the nets and the *father*" —"Go, sell all you have, give it to the poor, and follow me." And the two movements can end up in either liberation or thingification. The gospel sees the person in movement, in the movement of liberation. The ordinary, bourgeoise, vain woman who lives within the law which gives her the security of a home, a name, prestige, money, a circle of friends, is foreign to the gospel. The prudent woman, a good housewife who sews all day, who many nights lies awake waiting for children to come home, who washes and irons the clothing of the husband so that he will keep his standing in the tribunals of the great of the land, has remained locked in the Old Testament. I do not wish to cast a shadow of irony over this kind of woman who is so like so many of our own mothers. And certainly the women's liberation movement has a way of insinuating itself here. And it is not my intention to hold up, as an ideal of women's liberation, not the "woman of the house" but rather the woman who lives totally "outside," who aspires to automated motherhood, the automated kitchen, automated love, and the destruction of everything in which our fathers found poetry, psychic equilibrium, the joy of living. No, the gospel is not concerned with the order of things related to the structure of the family, strictly hierarchized by law and custom. The law has made man the master and woman the obedient one. It has made man sentimental and tender in the home and a thief outside of it. This taken-for-granted, comfortable "tenderness" has to be revised, judged anew, because it has the appearance of love but it is not love.

To hold that Jesus demands that woman sin is blasphemy. This is exactly the thesis of some romantic authors of the nineteenth century who were using the gospel for inspiration. The gospel describes the "poor" woman. Perhaps her true mission is to keep restlessness alive in the world, to destroy the "satisfaction" of man. Man is content with little: A few toys will distract him from his real problems. The trouble is that these toys have become dangerous—and perhaps they had to become dangerous so that the women, the youth, the poor, the threatened, would wake up. Woman's great responsibility in this situation is her having ceased to judge man, contenting herself with waiting for him in some little corner, dazzled by a glory that is hers only by reflection.

So the woman of the gospel is the unsatisfied one. We cannot, of course, identify her with a woman of the feminine liberation movement. For the liberation of women is not so much a political issue as one that bears upon a profound truth. It is separate from any historical phenomenon that might come close to it, such as the labor movement or the class struggle. But it goes to the heart of the problem. Woman's thirst is not for freedom but for a great deal of true love, for internal oneness—that is, liberation from plurality. Perhaps our generation will never fully understand the richness contained in the message of women's liberation because our problems are too complex for us to be able to hierarchize the themes of our culture and see them with clarity. Our reflection on this episode of the uninvited woman leads us to conclude that woman is poor, impoverished by man. He reduces her to plurality and ruins her. This "ruination" is the price that makes him an accomplice in the woman's refusal to make certain decisions.

Woman represents the polemic against the "satisfaction," the "self-sufficiency," and the "spiritual laziness" of the male. She must emerge from "plurality" to rediscover oneness, *the one thing necessary*. She has been entrusted with the mission of rediscovering life's true values; for this reason she easily succumbs to vanity, to getting lost in a multiplicity of things. Her very frailty is an indication that this is the vital point of her being. She can free herself only if she is attracted, and shaken out of herself, by a great love. And this love issues in the discovery of man in order to "consecrate him unto death." Women's liberation is inevitably bound up with the liberation of the poor, the struggle for justice.

Although I do not believe that a forward step in history, a transformation of the social structure, would automatically change the man-woman relationship, I can say with conviction that it seems out of the question even to talk about women's liberation in a static society that has yet to be universally liberated. The capitalist society is dynamic, but not along the lines of liberation. It provokes strong movements of liberation as dialectical antithesis, as opposition; and in this sense it could be a culture of liberation. Nevertheless I am convinced that to talk about women's liberation in a bourgeois context, to separate it from the liberation of the world's oppressed, is to perpetuate an illusion and waste time. Women's liberation is not freely given by man—no liberation is ever instigated by the oppressors—and neither is it liberation in the abstract. It should end in the "consecration unto death," that is, in the concrete commitment to give one's life for a broader liberation. The industrial and capitalist society collaborates in exposing the slavery and oppression of woman since, with its complicated structure, it cannot do without her. But it is powerless to liberate her. It creates a tremendous frustration for her which it tries to cover up with ever new projects. But the projects are static, because the planners are thinking "inside the house," in the hypothesis that the world is socially static. There is a pretense of changing a relationship within the general framework of "relationships that must not change." And that is absurd.

We arrive at the conclusion that women's liberation can be attained only within a global liberation, and that therefore the poor, those despoiled by man's power, are the true liberators—or, better still, are the axis on which all liberations spin off. Moreover, women's liberation can be frustrating if women do not take an active part in it. And they can share this commitment to freedom with men only if men are not playing at risk, at emotion; if for them the struggle is not an avoidance of the true purpose of life—a simple explosion of repressed instincts—but on the contrary a response to their true identity, to the authentic reason for living, to the demanding discovery of the real reason for their being in the world. And here I think we meet again with the absolutely Other, with him through whom every kind of otherness takes the form of the absolute and the necessary.

The danger confronting women's liberation is that of not being open to otherness, but on the contrary locking the self in the self and enclosing the other in a self that suffers from pathological loneliness. Our destiny is tragic. Injustice, exploitation of the person, frustration, loneliness—they all urge us to search for, and open ourselves to, the divine otherness and human otherness; and all the while our restless self defends itself, fails to find the road to otherness, and draws up plans for liberation that are static. They seem to be rich in concepts, reasons, and values. But fundamentally they are static and narcissistic, and are therefore condemned to inefficacy.

I would like to direct this thought especially to my Latin American friends, who have taught me to think deeply about liberation and discover the meaning of life in it. It seems impossible to them that their chosen course might end up, not too long from now, in the same swamp as capitalism. They think they will be saved because they try to avoid the obstacles of European intellectualism and American overorganization. Christ and the gospel seem, in their cultural context, like obstacles to liberation and, according to the best hypothesis, like an alien element that occasions the loss of time and the dissipation of energy. As for the kind of emptiness that technology has produced in the people of the rich countries, they regard it as intimately bound up with a culture this continent has repudiated, one which could not, therefore, cross over the frontiers into the Third World. To the extent that this emptiness is present here, it represents the residue of a historical stage that they intend to destroy as part of a process of creating something new and unheard of.

My own thought is that the great message of this continent would come from the discovery of Christ, not as a value apart from or beyond the theme of liberation but within it. My faith in Christ strengthens me and gives me peace, because if the liberation movement is truly a search for the human, it will lead the person searching for liberation to encounter with the others and the Other.

The sad problem remains of "the men who preferred darkness to light"—characteristic of people, of any person. It is the sorrow with which the whole of creation and of history groans, and it helps me to enter into the terrible mystery of the Cross and to understand it a little.

9

The Children of the Desert

My being proclaims the greatness of the Lord,
    my spirit finds joy in God my savior,
For he has looked upon his servant in her lowliness;
    all ages to come shall call me blessed.
God who is mighty has done great things for me,
    holy is his name;
His mercy is from age to age
    on those who fear him.
He has shown might with his arm;
    he has confused the proud in their inmost thoughts.
He has deposed the mighty from their thrones
    and raised the lowly to high places.
The hungry he has given every good thing,
    while the rich he has sent empty away.
He has upheld Israel his servant,
    ever mindful of his mercy;
Even as he promised our fathers,
    promised Abraham and his descendants forever
                      (Lk 1, 46–55).

The canticle attributed to Mary is a résumé of the Bible: Everything is in it. There is the implacable polemic against economic wealth and against the self-sufficiency of those who, sure of themselves, put teaching aside. There is the total renunciation of security for the sake of the greatest security we can find: that which does not come from goods and values—stepchildren of space and time—but is to be found on a historical plane that transcends the personal level, and for this very reason has the sign of infallibility and of the concrete. In this security the person, freed of chimeras, of self, of fear, of the unreal, and given over to total poverty, enters into a history that will necessarily be salvation history.

Mary gives the name "Lord" to the one who is all-powerful, the one who takes her to place her within the great sweep of history. A friend of mine, who is an atheist, does not accept the name "God" because he sees it associated with obscene covenants. But he understands Mary, carried along by history and forever joined to the process of salvation. My friend liberated himself by the absurdity of entering into a time of hope that was not his time and into a space that absorbed his space.

The theme of this chapter centers on two points: "He deposed the mighty and raised up the lowly; he gave the hungry every good thing and the rich he has sent empty away." This is the leading idea of Luke's gospel, its leitmotif. We are left perplexed by the thought that the church declares Mary to be its model, wishing to reproduce her in its lifestyle, and yet the church that people see the most of and talk most about is on the side of the "mighty" whom God means to depose and the "proud" whom God means to confuse. But here and there signs appear, little breakthroughs of a hidden church within the church, like the luscious fruit inside a rind that is much too thick. These breakthroughs are enough to give me hope and the courage needed to continue the struggle for the entry of the whole church into the perspective of Mary.

In 1972 an Argentine bishop wrote an unusual pastoral letter at Eastertime. It was addressed to a woman belonging to his diocese. I quote it here because I would never find a more exact translation into practice of what it occurs to me to call the "perspective of Mary":

As you know, every year I am accustomed to write a letter at Eastertime to the Christians of the diocesan church, as a brief message that might help them to reflect on the ever-present meaning of the Death and Resurrection of the Lord.

But this year I wish to make an exception, writing this letter to you which I will publish later. I would be very naive if I thought that in our diocese there were not at this moment a mass of people suffering a great deal. But your case is very special because it places in evidence what happens when someone commits herself to the cause of man, and above all because it demonstrates the value of Christian witness.

When they kidnapped you (there is no other name for what they did to you), your name did not make headlines. After all, you were just a lowly rural schoolteacher. . . .

At the same time, an attempt was made to fill the air with all kinds of calumnies that were believable to those who do not bother to look for truth at any source from which they could get a direct answer.

Fortunately, I well know the path you have taken, from the time you participated in a cursillo for rural teachers, eight or nine months ago, until your recent participation in the National Team of the Rural Movement, proceeding from your participation on the diocesan level, later in the Regional Secretariat of the Northeast, and still later at the Latin-American level—something that enabled you to learn about the misery of country people beyond our frontiers, as witness your letters to me from El Salvador and Guatemala.

For several weeks your family did not know your whereabouts, and a month went by before they got to see you.

Then it became known that you had been tortured. I confess that I found this hard to believe (after all, you were being held by the Second Army Corps) until I became convinced that the denunciation in the final document of the Synod of Bishops was about you also: "Well known are the cases of torture, especially involving political prisoners, who were often denied due process of law."

Today, a day in which we relive the love of Christ, it will have been four months since you were unjustly deprived of your liberty. It is easy to say "four months," but only you can know what this means, being aware of your innocence and of the abuses you are suffering.

On this day in which the Church reflects on the cowardly betrayal of Jesus and his imprisonment, how clearly it appears that *Christ continues to suffer in every human pain.* How palpable is the Passion of Christ in you who are living it in such a real and painful dimension. And at the same time how the words of our Lord are fulfilled in you: "Blessed are those who are persecuted for justice sake; the reign of God is theirs."

While I continue with negotiations to get you free, receive the embrace of the Resurrected Christ, conqueror of sin and death.

In this letter there are revealing signs of the presence of the church I am looking for: poverty, prophecy, martyrdom. That the above has to do with martyrdom there is no doubt, because the person to whom the letter is addressed has stated that only because of her faith has she been able to survive torture of a cruelty unworthy of the level of conscience we think we have reached. Prophecy illumines this tragic and obscene event, defining it as a stage of human liberation. This person belongs wholly to the oppressed, since there is nothing to justify the legal proceedings against her. The bishop who writes has been able to develop this sensitivity and to discover martyrdom in the only place it is to be found—that is, at this level of "worldly poverty"—because he is not just "in favor of the poor" or "protective" toward them but really lives with and among them.

It is true that church leaders should console everyone: Those who are suffering are no longer conquerors; they have been conquered. But the mistake many church leaders—indeed, the majority—make is one of *perspective:* We cannot judge events from two separate sides. The mighty who, in Mary's canticle, fall off their thrones, break their ribs and no one consoles them; and as for the rich, sent away empty and tragically tormented by this emptiness, no spiritual director will be able to offer anything to fill the void; the pains are double but the cause is single. There is just as much weeping and suffering in a luxury apartment as there is in a shack, but for the most part the cause of the suffering is to be found in the luxury apartment. If this fact is overlooked, going to weep with whoever is weeping in a sumptuous dwelling is unproductive for all. The mercy of God that reaches from generation unto generation is exactly what ruins the mighty and exalts the lowly. It is through this same mercy that those who believe themselves to be rich are found to be empty of the essential, of that which cannot be bought or inherited.

The Almighty is merciful when he exalts the lowly and is merciful when he knocks down the mighty. And he knocks them down not with a lightning bolt but with the vicissitudes of history that is made by people.

To understand this, to be just, we must share the condition of the oppressed, of the lowly, of the poor. This revelation, when seen from the side of whoever is currently powerful, is offensive and false. How clear it is to me that the gospel is not true, does not ring true, if its words are not pronounced from an existential situation that corresponds to them! Whoever has chosen to live by the gospel has chosen, as an inevitable consequence, to share the life of the most ignored and to see the world and history from their angle.

Today the problem that it behooves the church to solve is this: Its leaders know how to use the proper compassionate phrases to those who live in rank misery, or they are decently moved in face of epidemics, earthquakes, and injustice. Their words are just, but the position is mistaken, the focus unjust. In the kidnapping of an ambassador, all the powers of the earth spring into action and the church becomes the chancellery of any of these powers. The sensitivity of people of the church to events is manifested in judgments that are similar to those of other powers, and the press quotes them as saying things and making observations about the events that are opposite to what comes out of the mouths of those who are suffering and struggling to raise up the downtrodden. For one bishop who has the sensitivity to emphasize an episode of martyrdom and shame among the many things that happen in his diocese, there are ninety-nine who move heaven and earth over the kidnapping of an "important" person without asking themselves if, through this apparently unjust deed, the Almighty is not deposing the holders of power and exalting the lowly.

A zest for human beings, a passion for their good, the capacity for observing when and where their liberation is gestating, is not a problem of logic; it is the result of an option. We can only understand the history of the person with whom we live. From outside, compassion is a mockery and defense is demagoguery or cruelty.

The last thing to be understood is pain. And when it is understood, it is because there is friendship. Up till now the church has prepared leaders for a class of people not exactly poor. It has prepared ministers and evangelists from only one social sector, with the pretense that they are men of all classes. Those who go outside that class, the poor and the creative ones, cannot be understood by men of the church. It is not a question of bad will: The men of the church want to be everybody's friend. In fact, however, they are friends only of a certain class. Friendship is a problem of affinity, of living together, of participation in the creative act, in the movement of Exodus. The just concepts and messages of liberation rot away in the swamp of the middle class. In this ambience the canticle of Mary becomes so abstract that it loses all meaning. Only in a group that is on the move, that must achieve its liberation, that must discover the rights of the children of God, does the song sing of hope and promise for all.

Universal goodness, which does not really exclude anyone and includes all who suffer, can only be discovered and lived at the level of the oppressed, without leaving their side for an instant. If compassion and goodness give the oppressors the notion that they are victims, permit them to consider their pain as a justification, then compassion and goodness turn into injustice for them and for others. The song of Mary is a wave of compassion and of hope for all, and it vibrates with the pain of everyone because it is the song of one whom God has rescued from a static and pharisaic religion and put on the road to Exodus. It is an important sign that this song is put on the lips of Mary as she journeys toward a mountainous region.

God has not stooped down to a queen but to a poor and unlettered woman, and God has led her to discover the mercy that extends from generation unto generation in a world that rationalizes injustice and defends power with arms, even that most human and sensitive of arms, pain. The church has to remake itself in the image of Mary, rediscovering her song at the level of the poor and the oppressed. From that level it can become aware, without hatred or demagoguery, of the hurricane that is deposing the mighty from their thrones and exalting the lowly. If we could convince ourselves that this "partiality" (to the poor) becomes universality and that goodness is genuine only if it arises from this option, we would be free of the incoherence that cheapens our denunciations and emasculates our compassion. The letter quoted above is universal because it is partial. It exalts pain that is pure and that, with all the quantitative differences, is the pain of Christ —pain, consequently, in defense of people. In that letter there is not the slightest shadow of hatred or demagoguery, nor any discreet dissertations on justice and legality or endless analyses of the political situation. And its author is not someone who, fulfilling a duty, tangles things up with twists and turns to make all sides look good. He is a friend who suffers in the pain of the other, brutally kidnapped. The forthright and virile denunciation is at once loving and peacemaking. And he strikes out only at those who put obstacles on the road to liberation.

The strong and clear love that rings out from the notes of the *Magnificat* is unusual. So many hands have leafed through the gospel, so many dissertations have been given, that when somewhere the whitewash falls away and we see the bare stone, we become frightened. The sign that we are following the gospel and that we are not hearing the Word of God in vain is the coherence that arises from judging events from the angle of the oppressed.

I think that in our time the sign of the "devotee of Mary" is to have a zest for human beings, Mary's sense of humility, her live hope for change in the world. I have never been able to forget the unbelievable dialogue between a police official and a priest who had opted truly and consistently for the poor. The official said he was a "convert," and he was giving spiritual advice to the priest, suggesting that he should not get mixed up in problems of justice, which are too complex (problems of low salaries, eviction, lack of food). He was telling him: "Father, say fifty ejaculations a day to Mary, and everything will be OK." The gendarme felt obliged to blend his advice with a reminder about Mary, to fulfill his commitment as a "devotee." This mockery of the gospel that our words condemn is authorized by our incoherence.

In history Mary has appeared here and there with signs of the strength found in her song. The church has sensed her "terribleness," and at times has wielded this strength to combat enemies. In this stage of history, the heresy that winds its way through Latin America is the division of Christians into oppressors and oppressed; between those who hold on to wealth and power and those who, instead of being cherished, are beaten down by wealth and power. The profound division, a consequence of the unequal distribution of goods, has the countenance of heresy because generally the mighty call themselves Christians and pretend to come to the same table as the oppressed. Thus, in actuality, we have a phenomenon that has a distant analogy with Caesaropapism: The mighty defend their status with religion and pretend that those who threaten their property are enemies of religion.

The political structures, which have a strictly liberal origin, are clericalized in the extreme, and their newspapers are obedient parish bulletins. In defense of the existing order, a clerical front of opposition to any change has been created. Never in any place or at any time as here and now have there been so many spiritual retreats and so many weekends devoted to the problems of the soul. From these encounters a lot of orthodox people come forth, but very few sensitive to human needs. The episode cited above is neither strange nor unique. We are accustomed to hearing more sermons from a minister of state than from a bishop. No bishop has gotten after me to be faithful to prayer, to celibacy, to Marian devotion, in the way some of these generals and businessmen have. A person important on the national scene hangs up the telephone after getting the stock report to give me a commentary on a text of Saint John of the Cross that he read the night before.

It is clear that this interference with the intimate life of the priest is due not to "zeal for the glory of God," but to a desire to rein in the church and keep it linked up with power. In this comedy, which can have very amusing aspects, men who are leaders in the church are unfortunately accustomed to taking a part. Whether or not they are aware of the comedy is uncertain, but their naiveté certainly would have to be quite impressive, considering the responsibility they have taken upon themselves. A Benedictine prior tells me about a plan to reform the structure of the abbey according to which lots are to be distributed to members of the community who live around it. High officials of the Army are very interested in this plan, not because they are pleased with this step toward poverty and friendship, but because they want to prevent the venerable Benedictine tradition from being contaminated, from getting involved in "material" affairs. Generals who unsheath the rosary, businessmen who discuss theology, directors of banks who concern themselves with the eternal salvation of priests —all this agitation has only one objective: to control Christ and the gospel, so that the fire will not burn and send off sparks to kindle the liberation of the world.

Christians are becoming more dangerous now that they have discovered the gospel, and consequently the real and enormous power of the poor and their inalienable right to make and to judge history. To combat these dangerous Christians there are two methods: the Roman method that condemns them to the lions, to the cross, to forced labor; and the pharisaic method that consists in forcing them to compromise their faith—to show them that they are outside the line of Abraham, Isaac, and Jacob, to throw them out of the kingdom and damn them as sacrilegious. (I am sure that many priests who have abandoned their priestly commitment have done so because subconsciously there weighed upon them the bad conscience created by pharisaical persecution.) With this method they try to keep the world static, so that while there are "Christians" literally dying of hunger, other Christians increase their wealth in a geometrical progression.

The Third World is everywhere. It is not necessary to come to Latin America to find it, but here the situation is particularly sacrilegious. It is an outrage against the One who is called Providence, because the hatred hidden under the acceptance and spread of injustice is covered over with the gospel of Christ. Without any shame, young people in red ponchos embroidered with crosses declare themselves protectors of property. Where did the Bolivian workers come from who ward off hunger by chewing coca leaves, and the poor of Northeastern Brazil who nourish themselves with the worms that breed in the infested puddles of slum alleyways? Are they the fruit of the Providence of the Father who opens his hands and fills all creatures with good things, or are they products of "property"? Of the same property that the "new crusaders" defend with the rosary in one hand and a spear in the other, without discarding the notion of using guns later on. (It could be said that the Crusaders who went to rescue the Sepulcher of Christ were no less rapacious, but we ought to hope that the centuries have taught us something.) This is the great heresy of Latin America, the profound division in what, from certain aspects, could be called New Christendom.

All the studies of European theologians arrive here in gusts, but they do not stir up any temptation to heresy. Latin American theology is liberation theology, and it is at the heart of the Bible. The temptation against the faith is ever-present, certainly, and with every snare set. But no one is interested in the "how" of Christ's resurrection. In Latin America one has the impression that faith is an all-or-nothing matter. Here I feel history to be empty of ideology and full of humanity. From Europe it would be impossible to grasp this unique and unrepeatable phenomenon, to understand this "globality." Latin America is not a continent of primitives, or illiterates; it is something totally different. Here all the problems become *human*. Europeans who do not rid themselves of their Cartesianism and become converted to people, who do not accept this conversion from the intellectual to the existential—to the living, to the day-to-day—will always be alien to the Latin American continent. A short time ago, reading Michel Foucault, I felt my intuitions beginning to make sense in this stage I live in the history of Latin America.

> The fullness of history is not possible, except in the space that is empty and, at the same time, peopled by all the words without language that enable the sharp-eared to hear the quiet sound of voices from below, an obstinate murmur that must speak for itself, with no one to speak and no one in the self to answer, . . . a murmur that returns noiselessly to the silence from which it never departed.

Here the voice of history impoverishes us; it imposes silence upon us. It is significant, therefore, that the only way to stifle the cry of the poor is to deny history, deny the Exodus and, consequently, to deny the reality of Christ. This is the only great heresy of Latin America. The meter, discovered in Europe, cannot measure this earthy people that make history instead of projecting it. Every judgment coming from outside prescinds from reality. Here I have heard "those words without language" and "this quiet sound of voices that comes from beneath history," and I have better understood the *Magnificat*.

Mary, the chosen one of God, is not sundered from her people and its history; instead it is clear that she is grafted onto its roots. The manifestation of God to us is called incarnation, and the footprint of God is clear in this awareness of existing with others in history, that is to say, to exist as spectators and protagonists of happenings that change personal relationships and increase justice, love, and the ability to live peacefully in the world. For this reason contemplation, which is the consummate act of adoration of God, is not a flight into the clouds, an escape. It is, simultaneously, a vision of existing in faith and a profound, clear understanding of our existing in the world, in history. Anyone who feels liberated from the burden of being a person among people, from the responsibility of sharing the Exodus, should have doubts about having encountered God.

Where faith and adoration lead to political commitment, God makes himself present on this continent in a particular way. A person whose faith is divorced from commitment is a heretic. We cannot go astray in following the gospel, since the teaching church, which is the hierarchy, insistently, at least in word, presents a coherent vision of faith that leads to total commitment to humanity and to the struggle for justice. The living church is in the poor and oppressed. I have no polemical intention of separating things and making two churches. To be more precise, I would say that I cannot go wrong following the church that teaches through its hierarchy and makes me "acceptable" to the poor, at whose head walks the Lord Jesus.

Under the label of progressive and conservative—priests belonging to ecclesial renewal movements and priests resistant to all change—there are two visions of faith: The latter is without real roots, without real commitment to the world except the commitment to repression and rejection; the former is one that inspires concrete decisions for change and progress along the lines of justice. There is no power on earth that can change this process of renewal of the Christian faith that has exploded in our epoch.

The gift that Mary will make to this continent is to reveal the God who "has confused the proud in their inmost thoughts, deposed the mighty from their thrones and raised the lowly to high places." In few places on earth is Mary so much the center of attention and hope as in Latin America. From Guadalupe to Maipu I have seen huge masses of people crawling on their knees along interminable hard pavements to touch the statue of Mary and entrust to her their helplessness in the face of suffering. This ingenuous faith has brought home to me the gravity of the sin committed by those who abuse these people—their strength, their bodies, all that is human in them, all that has not been spent or corrupted by the cleverness of the conquistador that survives in the latter-day descendants.

The poor are discovering this image of Mary that the gospel gives us: the image that manages to inject into history a ferment of liberation, shaking the foundations of history and impressing upon it the rhythm of "depose the mighty and exalt the humble." Mary can purify the struggle for justice, in which the continent is engaged, of the hatred that is in everyone. She can give to this fierce and bloody struggle an objective that will not be the same old capitalist thing of providing a little more comfort without contributing to true human dignity. This new objective includes bread, work, housing, schooling, a share in the decision-making process, equal rights. Thus one would feel truly a person and would enjoy here on earth the pleasure and happiness that Christ proclaimed and intended for all.

The song of Mary is not "up in the air." It rises from the earth, out of a history bloodied by those who use power more for offense than defense of the right everyone has to essential goods. Nevertheless this voice that is lifted up from the earth and from history sings a song of joy. Every generation has a *right to happiness*, and every generation must gain it in a context of pain and struggle. Can one be carried away with joy and sing in a history that is full of trials and conflict? Yes, it is possible. But only on the condition that one is part of the Exodus history, of the attempt to transform the world. Only if one arrives at seeing that the promises God has made to us can be fulfilled. Only if one hears the current flowing strongly underground that contrasts with the seeming slowness of "there's nothing new under the sun." Only then is it possible to sing for joy.

This is the kind of evangelization that the church owes this Latin America that received a faith that was strange and foreign to its cultures. Here it is most *urgent* that the church rid itself of the cultural forms that are used to cover up injustice and oppression and rediscover the freshness of the song that introduces Him who "has a mighty arm," so mighty that no economic or military power can paralyze it. Here faith in God becomes a presage of liberation, a song of hope, a demand for political commitment. The jails are overflowing with men and women who fight for their brothers and sisters and for the liberation of the continent. Many shed their blood—sometimes as the victims of real savagery—for liberation. Of course, not everyone fights with the purity the gospel asks of us, but God is faithfully with his people on the march toward the promised land, and he does not abandon them even when they go astray or faint through weariness. "For the sake of the chosen, however, the days will be shortened" (Mt 24,22).

In the jails resplendent with martyrdom, the new Christian born in the defense of the neighbor receives the anointing of blood. In the face of this new kind of person, those who take refuge in a religious expression without roots in the land or in history, whether their motive is fear or self-interest, seems gross, anachronistic, "heretical." On the other hand, on the diplomatic level the plotting and search for alliances of politicians and men of the church takes on the appearance of scandal.

That the jails should be filled is the surest sign of hope, the clearest presage of a new world. "Philosophers have never changed the world"; martyrs change it. To suffer for others is, perhaps, the only reason for living. Prevented from loving directly because, in the normal development of our life, we grow up blocked off in the circle of self, we can love only in the painful act of suffering for others or laying down our life for them. In the deprivation of freedom, in the shameful profanation of their bodies, many discover that goodness which "extends from generation to generation." Some not too distant day, those who have suffered imprisonment and martyrdom will tell us of the joy they experienced in the midst of their sufferings, a joy they had not felt in the most jubilant of worldly celebrations. These men and women who know those sufferings and that joy are the pollen scattered over the land which will bring forth the new person—the person who suffers for others, who lays down his life for them and is reborn in a relation of brotherhood and love unknown until now. Then there will rise to the surface that "obstinate murmur that seeks to speak for itself," or better still, that "song that is born of silence and returns to silence, the calcified root of meaning."

The song of Mary is the song that goes to the heart of being chosen and loved by God, and therefore it is characterized by a sweetness, an optimism, a serenity comparable only to what we might have felt in a few rare moments of our youth; in those moments marked by the total absence of evil and of the "emptiness of history"—moments we ought always to remember in order to rise above those arid and gloomy intervals during which people and history seem to have turned against us.

If we have not plunged to the depths of this sea of being, if we have not felt ourselves in love with everything in such a way that nothing remains apart—separated—from us, we shall not be able to resist the waves of history. For the song rooted in this love and everlasting mercy becomes as threatening as a torrent that sweeps everything before it. The greater the vigor with which the projects of the proud—their insolent power, the security established by despising others—are resisted, the clearer will be the victory.

The song of Mary proclaims the terrible judgment of the dispossessed, the true and great victory of poverty, of weakness, of the Cross.